OPEN LEFT

OPEN LEFT

The Future of Progressive Politics

Andrew Gamble

policy network

ROWMAN &
LITTLEFIELD
—INTERNATIONAL—
London • New York

Published by Rowman & Littlefield International Ltd
Unit A, Whitacre Mews, 26-34 Stannary Street, London SE11 4AB
www.rowmaninternational.com

Rowman & Littlefield International Ltd. is an affiliate of Rowman & Littlefield
4501 Forbes Boulevard, Suite 200, Lanham, Maryland 20706, USA
With additional offices in Boulder, New York, Toronto (Canada), and Plymouth (UK)
www.rowman.com

British Library Cataloguing in Publication Data

A catalogue record for this book is available from the British Library

ISBN: PB 978-1-78660-908-3
    eBook 978-1-78660-909-0

Library of Congress Cataloging-in-Publication Data
Library of Congress Control Number: 2018945293

∞ ™ The paper used in this publication meets the minimum requirements of
American National Standard for Information Sciences—Permanence of Paper for
Printed Library Materials, ANSI/NISO Z39.48-1992.

Printed in the United States of America

CONTENTS

PREFACE

This book originated in a series of seminars organised by Policy Network during 2017 on the theme of the next progressive project for Britain. It was planned against a bleak outlook for centre-left progressive politics across Europe, following repeated election defeats in the years since the financial crash in 2008, the increasing strength of populist nationalists, Britain's vote to leave the EU in June 2016, and the election of Donald Trump in November 2016. The project was called Open Left because we wanted to invite a broad range of people from different backgrounds and institutions, those with particular party affiliations and those with none, and particularly people with different opinions about the way forward. We did not want to create yet another echo chamber. In the spirit of an Open Left we hoped everyone who attended would learn from the exchanges as we explored the many complex and perplexing problems which confront us.

This book does not attempt to be a summary of those discussions, but it draws on them, and sets out one vision of what an Open Left might be like and the kind of issues it should seek to confront. It does not seek to be comprehensive or encyclopedic. Many readers will disagree with some of the arguments and some of the priorities and emphases, and may question some of the omissions. But the book will have succeeded in its purpose if it provides a stimulus to further debate and exploration of the issues it raises.

Many of the problems and circumstances which confront progressives at the present time are common to all the western democracies and to many other states as well. In that sense this book addresses problems and raises themes which are general in scope. It also seeks to illustrate the argument by focusing on the circumstances, issues and problems which are specific to one particular country, in this case Britain. This is not because Britain is unique, or exceptional, or supremely important, in the way many Brexiteers imagine it to be. It is because it offers a window into a set of common problems, and hopes in that way to be a contribution to a more general conversation among those with a progressive disposition about how these challenges are being tackled in other countries.

In chapter 1 I discuss the present dilemmas and challenges facing progressives. Chapters 2, 3, 4 and 5 look at four substantive areas: security, the economy, welfare and democracy. Chapter 6 summarises the argument and explores the way ahead.

I would like to thank everyone at Policy Network for their help and encouragement with this book, and particularly Charlie Cadywould, Patrick Diamond, Matthew Laza and Roger Liddle, as well as the many people who attended the series of Policy Network seminars held in the second half of 2017 that have informed my thinking. I would also like to thank my colleagues and students at Sheffield, especially those at Sheffield Political Economy Research Institute, and at Cambridge for discussions over many years on the themes and issues raised in this book.

Policy Network has been a living embodiment of the ideals of an Open Left. It has promoted dialogue and discussion on progressive politics in a non-partisan and ecumenical spirit, and built networks across Europe and around the world. I have been very fortunate to have been involved in seminars and conferences which they have organised over many years and have learnt a great deal from the open intellectual exchanges they have fostered.

Andrew Gamble
April 2018

WHERE WE ARE

The years since the financial crash in 2008 have not been easy for progressive politics. Parties of the centre left, whether social democratic, green or social liberal, have lost ground and suffered defeats in almost all the major western democracies. In some cases, formerly successful progressive parties, like Pasok in Greece, have all but disappeared. In others, like the Dutch Labour party, they have lost the bulk of their support to new challengers. There have been some exceptions to this rule, particularly among new left parties such as Syriza in Greece, Podemos in Spain, and Jeremy Corbyn's Labour in Britain. But although they have brought a new energy to the left and some fresh ideas, none have yet shown that they have a viable programme for government or vision for society which could start to rebuild the fortunes of the progressive left across Europe and beyond.

Twenty years ago, at the height of the boom that followed the end of the cold war and the quickening pace of globalisation, the picture was very different. Centre-left parties were in office across most of the western democracies, including the US. The third way was in full swing, and its promise to combine economic efficiency with social justice through the policies of the social investment state proved widely popular. A new era of progressive centre left advance seemed to be unfolding. There was even talk of a progressive century. These parties and governments were working within the constraints of the new international order shaped by the doctrines of neoliberalism and the opportunities of globalisation, but they were demonstrating that there were practical alternatives to the kind of policies pursued by the Thatcher government and the Reagan administration in the 1980s.

This was a period of relative optimism and confidence that increasing political and economic cooperation could begin to solve some of the pressing problems with which the world was confronted, particularly on the environment, global poverty and nuclear proliferation. The rules-based international order, which had collapsed amid the economic slumps and military conflicts of the 1930s and 1940s, was rebuilt under US leadership after 1945 and, despite challenges and upheavals, particularly during the cold war and the stagflation of the 1970s, it had survived. With the collapse of the Soviet Union in 1991 and the increasing participation in the global economy of some of the world's most populous and poorest nations, especially China and India, a fresh beginning seemed possible. A new world order bringing all the nations of the world into economic and political cooperation within a single set of institutions and rules seemed to some within reach.

In the years that followed some progress was made towards this goal. The advance of China and India transformed the world economy, lifted millions out of extreme poverty, and changed perceptions of what the future of the world would be like. The old Eurocentric and western assumptions which had ruled for the previous two centuries were weakening. This was an optimistic time, a prosperous time and often an exhilarating time, but there were already dark clouds and a growing awareness that not all was well. There were repeated financial crises; problems in controlling the economic forces which globalisation had unleashed; the emergence of new ethnic conflicts in the former Yugoslavia and Rwanda; the rise of new terrorist organisations, most spectacularly al-Qaida with its attack on the US on 9/11; the intervention of the western powers in Afghanistan and Iraq; and the failure to integrate Russia as a full partner in the western international order. Liberal peace became liberal war.

Before the financial crash of 2008 there were already signs of darkening prospects. Many things were not going well. Populist nationalist movements were loudly pointing to what was wrong and campaigning against the political and economic elites they claimed were running the international system and trampling on the rights and interests of nations. But these movements have been amplified hugely since 2008. Today there is hardly a western democracy which does not have a vigorous challenge from a populist nationalist movement claiming to represent the 'will of the people', pitching the sovereign nation against the global elite. What was surprising was that the major breakthrough for the populist nationalists when it came was not in France, the Netherlands, or Italy but in the US, with the election of Trump in November 2016, and in the UK with the vote in the referendum earlier that year to leave the EU.

The rise of populist nationalism has been a key factor in the fading fortunes of the centre left. Its politicians found it hard to articulate a response to the financial crash and the austerity programmes which followed. Centre-left parties were seen by many voters as governing parties, part of the web of elites who were held responsible for the crash and the recession. Having been so long in government during the boom years centre-left parties found it hard to find a voice as outsiders and critics. That was something taken up with relish by the populists who delivered simple punchy messages about immigration, jobs and services, the iniquities of globalisation, and the loss of control to supranational bodies like the European commission.

The decade after the crash brought to the fore trends which had been building for some time. The traditional support base of centre-left parties in the working-class communities of the industrial heartlands has been in sharp decline. The restructuring of many advanced economies away from manufacturing towards services, which was a marked feature of the 1980s, further accelerated in the 1990s as jobs were outsourced by multinationals to low-cost producers such as China (Figure 1.1). There was a sharp reduction not only in the number of people employed in manufacturing but also in the numbers belonging to trade unions. Many of the institutions which had sustained an independent labour movement no longer appeared relevant in the new age of globalisation, and there was nothing it seemed that centre-left parties could do about it except press for programmes which gave some support to communities and allowed individual workers to retrain. Many workers still ended up in low-skill, temporary or precarious employment, with few rights and a loss of the status and self-respect they had formerly enjoyed. Many of them felt left behind and abandoned. As traditional loyalties gradually melted away many became attracted to the new direct messages of the populists.

At the same time as support among its traditional base was ebbing, the centre left was becoming more attractive to other groups of voters, winning over ever greater numbers of young, university-educated middle-class professionals and public sector workers. To win elections centre-left parties needed to keep both groups within their coalition, but after 2008 few of them managed to do so sufficiently. The centre left has had few answers to the new politics of identity developed so seductively by the populists. Class has not disappeared as a factor in voters' allegiances, but other political divides have

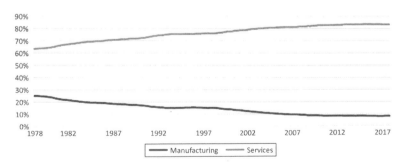

Figure 1.1 Workforce jobs in manufacturing and services in the UK, 1978–2017. *Source*: Office for National Statistics (ONS), Workforce Jobs by Industry, 1978–2017.

become more salient, centred particularly on age and education. Class has become less important in determining how individual citizens define their political identity.

In charting new directions for progressive politics we need to start from a realistic assessment of where we are and the obstacles that lie in the way of achieving progressive goals. Some of these obstacles are economic and political, some cultural. We should not exaggerate the threats we face, but nor should we underestimate them.

THREATS TO INTERNATIONAL ORDER

The multilateral, rule-based western international order has come under increasing attack since the 2008 financial crash. The crash highlighted the shifting balance in the world economy as the US, Europe and Japan all went into recession and struggled to recover while China, India and many other non-western economies continued to grow for a time at the same pace as before. From the beginning, the western international order had reflected US priorities and interests. A US-dominated order was the only liberal order on offer after 1945, and the more radical ideas of John Maynard Keynes and others for institutions which might more directly pursue the global public good were quickly ruled unacceptable by the US. The prize of multilateral and increasingly open trade was won but on US terms. In return for its undisputed primacy over its allies the US made concessions in its governance of the international system to ensure that the countries devastated by the second world war, including the defeated nations, were able to recover, and a remarkable period of prosperity, *Les Trente Glorieuses*, was the result.

But that phase of development, partly as a result of US policies, ended in the collapse of the international monetary system agreed at Bretton Woods in 1971. The US then moved to reconstruct the international order in ways which more directly reflected its national interests. The stagflation of the 1970s and the restructuring it necessitated was painful but eventually the obstacles were overcome and a new period of advance began, leading eventually to a new boom, not as impressive, at least for the western democracies, as the postwar boom, but still substantial. This period ended with the financial crash of 2008.

A new restructuring is needed today, but the task is greater than in the 1970s. The position of the US has changed, and it is no longer either able or willing to play the role which it once did. Under Trump there has been a revival of the slogan America First. US administrations after 1945 were always concerned to put America first but they identified the US interest with the preservation and extension of the liberal world order they had built. By giving voice to the angry anti-globalisation protests of those US regions which feel excluded and disrespected by the liberal cosmopolitan elites of the corporate, financial and media worlds, Trump is setting the US against the multilateral rule-based economy which has underpinned western prosperity since 1945. Under Trump, the US is turning its back on many of the multilateral institutions it took such trouble to create, and is instead favouring bilateral deals. How far this may go is still uncertain, but there have already been several symbolic gestures – such as the refusal to participate in the Trans-Pacific Partnership, withdrawal from the Paris climate change agreement, and an enthusiasm to embark on trade wars.

This willingness of the US to disengage is a sign of weakness rather than strength. It is because the US is no longer able to remake the world order on its own terms that elements of US opinion, noisily articulated by Trump, are in favour of giving up leadership and retreating to a more isolationist position. The alternative would be for the US to agree a sharing of power and control with some of the rising powers, particularly China and India, leading to a reconstruction of the governance of the international order to make it less centred on the west, but there is very little appetite for that at the moment in Washington. Even the adjustment of voting weights on the board of the International Monetary Fund (IMF) to give China a greater say was held up for several years by the US Senate.

Without the renewal and deepening of the multilateral rules-based order, one of the fundamental building blocks for a progressive politics and progressive movements is missing. This is not only about economic prosperity. It is also about finding ways to deepen cultural exchanges and political cooperation for the many challenges which cross national borders. Climate change and nuclear proliferation are two great existential threats to humankind. If they are to be met successfully then greater multilateral cooperation not less will be needed. Currently such cooperation is weak, and urgently needs to be strengthened. This has to be one of the key aims for an Open Left.

THREATS TO EQUALITY AND INCLUSIVENESS

A second concern is the threat posed to inclusive economies and advanced welfare states, which, although imperfect and often attacked, remain the proudest achievements of generations of progressive politicians in western democracies. This threat arises because of the trends towards growing inequality that was an outcome of the political economy which came to dominate western economies in the two decades before the crash, and because of the effects of the crash itself on living standards. Proponents of globalisation often claimed that it was successful precisely because it helped to weaken many of the protections and institutions in national democracies which had made *Les Trente Glorieuses* such an important period of progressive advance. Parties of the centre left had to adjust to the new constraints and find new ways to advance progressive aims in the new economic and political landscape. Substantial gains were registered across Europe, but to many critics it seemed that the successes of the different variants of the third way were secured only by abandoning basic principles and accepting the new commonsense about the primacy of markets and the limited role of the state.

A key part of progressive politics has always been how to ensure an expanding and prosperous economy, one which benefits all citizens. Without prosperity, all progressive objectives become much harder to achieve, and it is a melancholy fact that progressive parties have rarely thrived during times of economic adversity. Since the 2008 crash the slowness of the recovery, and the worries about productivity and living standards, have raised anxieties that the western economies may be stuck in a long period of poor economic performance. That performance, it is feared, will make any kind of creative progressive politics more difficult, fuel anti-system populist movements and scapegoat immigrants and other minorities. Many explanations have been put forward as to why the economy is so sluggish. Every upturn has been heralded as the return to normality, but so far each upturn has proved short-lived. The headwinds against economic growth have proved too strong.

At the heart of the dilemma is the productivity puzzle. Despite the ever-quickening pace of technological innovation, productivity has been stuck, and because productivity has failed to rise so have wages for the majority. These trends existed before the financial crash but in its aftermath they have been put into much sharper relief. Many factors seem to be responsible including flexible labour markets and the weakening of trade unions, the ease with which capital flows across borders, and the increasing reluctance of states to impose regulation on successful business sectors.

Another long-term trend has been the rise in inequality in western economies. Inequality across the world has fallen in the last three decades, mainly because of the astonishing rates of growth achieved in China and India, and many other poor countries, and that has been a major progressive change which globalisation has brought about. But in the western world, and particularly but not exclusively in the Anglo-Saxon world, inequality began increasing again, returning to the kind of levels that existed in the 19th century, before the progressive reforms which culminated in the reformed capitalism of the second half of the 20th century. The economist Branko Milanovi has shown that for the world as a whole between 1988 and 2011 the bottom groups in the global income distribution did relatively poorly, but the global middle classes did relatively well particularly in China. Those between the 45th and 65th global percentiles doubled their income. But the middle-income groups in the rich countries had stagnant real incomes, while the global top 1% had real income increases of 40%.

Under New Labour, the growth of income inequality in the UK slowed markedly as a result of policies such as the minimum wage and Sure Start children's centres. The financial crash also meant that for a time income inequality ceased to grow at all and even went into reverse. But because so many of the policies to combat poverty were abandoned in the implementation of austerity, this was not expected to last. Trends to increasing inequality of wealth proved much harder to counter throughout the globalisation era. Once austerity and retrenchment took hold, the gulf between rich and poor, and the cumulative effect of such a long period of stagnant real incomes for middle-income groups, fueled resentment and added to popular rage against elites.

A further challenge is protecting the welfare state, which has increasingly come under attack as unaffordable and inefficient. Periods of austerity generally see retrenchment of public expenditure and swings of opinion against welfare recipients. But support for universal entitlements continues to be strong. The problem faced by progressives is how to combine reforms to how the welfare state is organised to make it more responsive to citizens' needs, while persuading the same citizens to pay higher taxes to fund the quality of services they say they want. Welfare states were signal achievements of progressive parties, which have always been their strongest defenders. But since the 1970s welfare states have been subject to sustained ideological and political attack, questioning why the state has to be involved at all in the provision of welfare. A new assault on the universalism of the welfare state has emerged. At the same time, not all claimants have been treated the same in the politics of austerity. In the UK particular benefits have been cut, not all benefits. The young were particularly targeted with the cutting of benefits for people of working age and families, and the trebling of university student fees, while pensioners' benefits were protected. This generational divide once opened becomes difficult to close.

The challenge facing a progressive political economy in these times is formidable. We have to find a new economic model which can revive prosperity in order to meet the aspirations of citizens for a rising standard of living and to restore funding to public services squeezed to breaking point by austerity. At the same time, we have to cope with the growing risks to the environment which established modes of economic activity are causing. Can this be done? The scientific evidence all stacks up one way. We are facing potentially irreversible changes to our planet brought about by climate change, loss of biodiversity, and the acidification of the oceans. In countering global warming we have only limited time – scientists estimate no longer than three decades, until 2050 – to bring down the current use of seven tonnes of CO_2 equivalent per person to only two tonnes per person, to avoid reaching a tipping point. If world economic growth recovers to its previous levels on the old lines, then the scale of adjustment becomes even greater. The changes to our economy, society and behaviour implied by these numbers are immense. The question becomes not just how can we move to a form of economy which is sustainable for the long run, but should we, at least in the rich western democracies, be aiming for zero growth? And, if that is our conclusion, how can we begin to make that a viable politics that can win majority support?

THREATS TO PLURALISM AND DEMOCRACY

It is not as though our democracies are in very good shape. In the 1990s there was considerable optimism about the future of democracy. The breakup of the Soviet Union after the end of the cold war created many new democracies in east and central Europe. After the end of apartheid in South Africa, and of several military dictatorships in South America, by 2000 the number of states that met the tests for democracy had risen to the highest level it had ever been. Of the 195 member states of the UN, 117 were classified as electoral democracies. Sixty years before, in the midst of world war and before the creation of the UN, there were just 12. This was a cause for great celebration, and gave rise to the hope that democracy might become the standard to which all states would aspire. But this optimism has not lasted and in the first two decades of the new century a much more troubling prospect has emerged. Several states, including Russia and Turkey, have moved in an increasingly authoritarian direction and, although they have retained some of the formal trappings of democracy, have become democracies in name only, at best illiberal democracies, with widespread disregard for human rights. This taste for authoritarian rule has spread to many parts of the world, fueled by the populist nationalist insurgencies. This has come to affect even the EU, where some of the new member states, particularly Hungary and Poland, have moved in this direction, but it is also affecting some of the older member states, with the nationalists now in coalition in Austria, and close to power in Italy after the 2018 elections. Democracy appears to be in retreat again, with the number of states that meet the criteria for democracy beginning to decline. The election of a populist nationalist president in the US confirms the trend. Trump is constrained by the checks and balances still present in the US system, but his distaste for rules and due process, his disparaging of facts and expertise, and his praise for authoritarian leaders including Vladimir Putin and Xi Jinping, make him a potent symbol for the new regressive politics.

These trends are occurring alongside declining trust in politicians and the institutions of representative government in western democracies. They predate the 2008 financial crash but, again, have been greatly amplified by it. The feeling has grown that politicians are no longer representative in the way they once were, that parties are no longer rooted in the communities of civil society, and that there is a political class – comprising most of the politicians from all the mainstream parties – which has become increasingly distanced from the citizens they represent and serve. This has been fueled by major scandals such as the UK parliamentary expenses scandal in 2009, but more generally by the belief that politicians are only in it for themselves, that they will say anything to get elected, and that voting does not make a difference. Whoever is in office the same policies are pursued and nothing changes. There has always been a significant part of democratic electorates which has felt like this, and there have been populist insurgencies before. The question today is whether these attitudes are becoming majority attitudes, or close to majority attitudes, in several western democracies and whether this will lead to the election of more charismatic populists whose political instincts are authoritarian, nationalist and deeply hostile to institutions of liberal democracy. These authoritarians still claim the mantle of democracy, but it is a new kind of illiberal democracy they seek. The Russians call it sovereign democracy. It means a democracy without checks and balances on the executive – no free press, no effective rule of law and no protection for minorities, freedom of speech or free association.

There are deeper problems underlying this. The model of representative democracy itself is under attack. There is growing support even in some of the longest-established democracies for plebiscites. If the elected representatives no longer represent anyone except themselves or sinister vested interests, then consulting the people directly through referendums or online polling, it is suggested, might produce better government. In the past it was an old assumption of radical politics that the people are asleep but the interests are always awake. Many radicals wanted to wake the people, but the purpose was mostly to elect representatives to parliament who would more faithfully reflect the people's interests. The call now is to bypass the representatives and seek direct consultation of the people.

This call has been aided by the growth of new media platforms such as Twitter, Facebook, Google and YouTube, which have rapidly transformed political possibilities and political assumptions and forced all political actors to confront some new political realities. These include the polarisation of debate, the creation of online communities that seek out information which confirms their existing beliefs, the habit of calling everything with which you disagree 'fake news', and the relativising of knowledge and truth, so that all points of view become equally valid and deserving of a hearing, even when they are manifestly false. Defenders of the new media argue that all these things existed before, which is true, but the intensity and immediacy is different. The accessibility of the new media and the speed with which messages can be disseminated has added a new dimension. The internet and the new media initially appeared to offer greater pluralism and diversity in new sources and new ways for people to communicate in decentralised and non-hierarchical ways. They still do, but as the internet revolution has proceeded so its more negative aspects have also become apparent, and the threat to the public domain as an independent and impartial space, which promotes the common good and protects the common interests of all citizens, has grown.

The new media has not created the new identity politics but it has helped to solidify the new alignments and polarisation that has occurred. It has made it easier for national communities and national cultures to be fragmented and divided. Once politics becomes more a matter of identity rather than interest compromises are harder to find, politics becomes less concerned with a pragmatic search for the best policies based on evidence, and more about the politics of affirmation, entertainment and spectacle. None of these trends are new in democracies. However, the rise of social media amid the perceived failure of the political class after the financial crash to deliver a lasting recovery, or to deal with issues like immigration, has opened the door to outsider insurgencies. Their aim is to challenge the institutions of liberal democracy, particularly the rule of law and due process, the separation of powers, the equal rights of all citizens, and international cooperation with other states.

THE WEAKENED CAPACITY OF THE STATE

There is a fourth threat which must be added to the problems of agreeing new rules for governance of the international trading order, reorienting the economy to sustainable and inclusive growth, and rebuilding trust and legitimacy in democratic institutions. Progressive projects of right and left in the last 200 years have relied on the state as a crucial agency to deliver the kind of change they want to see. The state is larger and more pervasive than ever before, but its capacity to act coherently is diminished. There is a growing list of problems which are difficult to solve and for which state capacities seem inadequate. These include climate change, nuclear proliferation, international migration, terrorism and new diseases. In recent years there has been a growing pessimism about the state and public action. In some earlier periods in the 20th century there was boundless confidence in the capacity of the state to solve problems. It was the engine of choice for all who wanted to effect change. Not any more. The state has come to be seen as overextended, inflexible, overburdened, indecisive and hard to coordinate. Because the problems the state faces are so complex the solutions have to be as well, but that is difficult to sell to democratic electorates who have come to expect instant gratification of their wants and are easily swayed by the slogans and promises of the populists.

If the state cannot solve these problems, what can? Voluntary action, markets, corporations or other civil society institutions have all been suggested. All are important in different contexts but no one is confident that they are sufficient without the enabling, steering, coordinating functions that states can supply when at their best. Populist nationalists are also seeking change but they have the easier task. They are seeking more closed societies. They want the state to do more but to do things which are very familiar, like imposing tariffs or building walls, shutting down immigration or stockpiling more weapons. The progressive agenda is harder to deliver because progressives want to see more open, inclusive and egalitarian societies. To do this they need to build institutions and networks which will foster and sustain cooperation, while retaining domestic political legitimacy.

A NEW PROGRESSIVE PROJECT?

The problems and threats standing in the way of a new progressive project are real enough, but counsels of despair and fatalism are overdone. Politics in times like these is very fluid and the uncertainties about what the future may hold particularly high. But then modernity has always been like this. It generates optimism and pessimism in almost equal measure. It is hard to find any solid ground from which to form a balanced assessment of what is happening and what is likely to happen. Against the rising tide of nationalist and populist anger progressives need to be resolute. There are many ways to fight back and many resources to mobilise.

The project for an Open Left is one of these. It seeks an open multilateral international order that is no longer focused primarily on the western democracies, an inclusive and sustainable economy, a remodelled welfare state, and a renewed democracy. These might seem quite modest ambitions, but in present circumstances they can also seem wildly ambitious. But they are not utopian. A viable progressive project needs to draw on utopian thinking to imagine possible futures. But it also has to avoid setting completely unrealistic goals. We have to understand as well as possible the context in which we are operating and the realities and constraints we face. The following chapters will seek to address these, but first it is necessary to say something on what it means to call a political project 'progressive'. Like left and right, or democratic, progressive is a term much abused and distorted, and its meaning is often slippery. All manner of political movements and parties have called themselves progressive. The number of parties and movements happy to call themselves reactionary or regressive has dwindled. On the political spectrum it is hard to find genuine reactionary parties who seriously want to dismantle the structures and institutions of the modern world. In that sense we are all progressives now.

But although the term progressive covers such a wide spectrum it does have a core meaning, which explains why so many on the left in every generation have considered themselves progressives. It entails a belief in progress, or at least the possibility of progress, in human affairs, specifically the type of progress associated with modernity in the last 200 years – the dramatic acceleration of output, productivity and population; the raising of health and education standards and life expectancy; the movement of the world's population from the land into cities; the switch from agriculture to industry, services and now the digital economy; the lifting of drudgery; the increase in free time. The changes have been so dramatic and rapid that the modern era is already separated sharply from all the eras that came before it. It is a break in human history comparable only to the transition from hunter-gathering to agriculture and the creation of cities and states. This modern era is still so recent and such a short time in human experience that it is hard to see it in perspective. There have always been critics of progress who wanted to stop it altogether. They have been defeated by a coalition of those who have broadly supported the changes. The belief in progress implies that human societies are capable of being improved. The more hubristic claim is that human beings, if they choose, can become controllers of their fate, by embracing reason and science, the experimental methods of trial and error, and gradually and patiently refining and improving knowledge on the basis of evidence and experience. Over time this has led to a radical transformation of society, economy, politics and culture. Progressives in this sense have often disagreed over the means, but they have been united in seeing the changes as on balance positive and leading to greater opportunity, prosperity and wellbeing for all.

The history of the modern era has been far from smooth. Progress has always been uneven and often won at huge cost. There have been devastating wars, oppressions, famines, economic depressions and displacement of peoples. There has often been a sense too of a world that no one controls or could control, that human beings in their hubris and arrogance have unleashed forces that are beyond them. These are the themes of the very powerful strains of cultural pessimism which have always accompanied progress at every stage and are shared by many on the left today. Yet the achievements and improvements of the last two centuries are both remarkable and measurable. To be a progressive in politics is to acknowledge as much. But that should not stop progressives from being critical of many aspects of the modern world. Realism and pragmatism are needed, rather than any kind of Panglossian optimism. The situation for most people in the world has measurably improved over the last two centuries, but there is still a long way to go, and there are always new dangers which threaten what has been achieved. Progress is never guaranteed. It can go into reverse and, at times in the last two centuries, it has.

This book champions the cause of an Open Left. Such a project can be advanced by many different political parties and movements. Progressives have always had a dilemma as to which party was most likely to carry forward a progressive agenda, and this is perhaps particularly true at the present time when many old loyalties have broken down and the dominance of class politics has faded. Many different parties and movements now make up the centre left in western democracies – green, liberal, social democrat and socialist. They are not the only ones who support the idea of progress. There are parties on the centre right that do so as well, although with different emphases and priorities. To be a progressive and on the left means attaching a high priority to promoting equality, autonomy and security for all human beings. Those on the centre right often disagree with the centre left on means, and this conflict over means between centre left and centre right still defines a great deal of contemporary politics. But there are elements, particularly on the right, who reject progress and democracy. These reactionary elements were once much stronger and more effective, and in some countries and cultures they remain so. But the main threat to western democracies lies not in the reactionary elements, but in the new populist nationalists who set themselves against the existing political order and liberalism.

The rise of populist nationalism is a reminder of the fragility of political orders, and that the institutions which have provided peace, prosperity, happiness and wellbeing can easily be undermined and even discarded. To be a progressive in politics has always meant to support democracy, in the sense of extending civil, political and social rights to all. The content of these rights, and the priority to be given to particular rights, has shifted over time, but not the central importance given to achieving an order that respects and protects the rights of individuals. Some argue that the progressive attitude and the progressive inheritance is deeply rooted in the tradition of the European Enlightenment in the 18th century, with its emphasis on reason and humanism, which aided the development of those three pillars of modernity – capitalism, science and democracy. The centre left has tended to give greater emphasis to science and democracy while the centre right has given more weight to science and capitalism. A tension between liberalism and democracy has always been present, and the different emphasis continues to form one of the great dividing lines between right and left. But it should not be exaggerated. All mainstream parties have accepted the goals of a thriving economy which can deliver prosperity, a creative science which can drive innovation and policy, and a substantive democracy which can provide accountable government and the protection of rights and the rule of law.

Enlightenment values and principles have always had their critics, and the recent resurgence of economic nationalism, cultural illiberalism and political authoritarianism is only the latest manifestation of this. But it is important to recognise that a politics guided only by Enlightenment values can also be criticised from a progressive standpoint as too Eurocentric, too concerned with one kind of knowledge and truth, too concerned with measurement and calculation to understand the importance of other values, knowing the price of everything but the value of nothing. An Open Left has to offer more than the desiccated calculating machines of modern bureaucracies, important though those are for certain purposes. There also has to be a passion and a commitment to people where they are, in their communities, with their particular identities and peculiarities. An Open Left has to speak to them and for them as well.

The counter-Enlightenment of the 19th century spawned many regressive and reactionary movements, but also contained important lessons for progressives, and its insights have been used by progressives as different as John Stuart Mill and Karl Marx, Karl Polanyi, RH Tawney and Edward Thompson. The Romantic tradition probed deeply ideas of belonging, identity and community, many of which were under serious attack from some of the forms that progress assumed. Recognition of the costs as well as the benefits of the growth of industries and cities, and the need to counter new harms and provide protection and compensation for those suffering the consequences of rapid social change, have always been part of the progressive critique of modernity, and in developing that critique the insights from the Romantic tradition need incorporating. An Open Left has to be concerned with issues of place and identity as well as international cooperation and global networks, and give a greater priority to relationships and communities, families and households than the profit and loss calculations of faceless state and corporate bureaucracies A false polarisation is growing up in which economic nationalists are being counterposed to globalists, nativists to cosmopolitans. We should reject it. We can be citizens of the world, like Socrates, and at the same time citizens of particular nations, cities and communities. We can even, for a little longer if we are British, be citizens of the EU. There is no contradiction, and suggesting otherwise is stupid, and plays into the hands of the populist nationalists. That is what they want us to believe.

As an Open Left we need to abandon the idea that one tradition of progressive thought has all the answers. We need openness to new policy ideas, and openness to learning from past mistakes and the experience of others. We should be prepared to listen to very different voices and draw from very different intellectual traditions, including some of those we instinctively reject. We should engage with people from a wide range of communities and backgrounds. The last thing an Open Left should do is retreat from the world. We need a dialogue with progressive movements from many different countries, learning from their experiences of putting progressive ideas into action.

The idea of progress is still a noble one, but it needs updating. Future progress is not guaranteed. The challenges we face may be no greater than some of those faced in the past but they are in certain respects novel, and we need to be open-minded, pragmatic and realistic in facing them.

SECURITY

The modern world system can be traced back several centuries, and there have been huge changes in that time, particularly in the last 200 years. But what has not changed is the fundamental character of the system. It has always combined a tendency towards increasing economic interdependence with the fragmentation of political authority into separate sovereign jurisdictions. Finding ways to reconcile those two has never been easy, and it is a key issue for an Open Left. The dilemma can be simply stated. An Open Left, as the name implies, is committed to the principle of an open, multilateral, international order, which is no longer western-centric but remains rules-based and facilitates the greatest possible degree of cooperation and exchange between nations. At the same time, in order to succeed progressive parties must win support within every nation state. They must persuade their voters that the security of the nation – military, economic and cultural – can be achieved best by engaging with the rest of the world rather than putting up barriers to it. This sets up a tension, which populist nationalists have been quick to exploit.

In 2018 the world is awash with economic nationalism and cultural nationalism. There are calls to close borders, build walls, send immigrants home, fight trade wars, protect local industries and reverse decades of economic cooperation. Nationalists want to take back control and restore national sovereignty and national independence, ending multilateral international agreements, and only engaging in bilateral negotiations with other states. An Open Left is instinctively opposed to all this, but can it fight it? The advance of the nationalists seems inexorable, the vote for Brexit, the election of Trump, the entry of the nationalists into many European governments – Poland, Hungary and Austria. The World Trade Organization (WTO) is deadlocked, multilateral trade agreements are collapsing, and states are once again giving priority to the pursuit of their own national interest, whatever wider damage this may cause. The growing conflict and tensions are an unhappy reminder of a much darker time, the 1930s. The western international order is much stronger than it was then, but its survival is not guaranteed, especially now that the state which did more than any other to establish it after 1945 seeks to disengage, and in some ways to repudiate its own achievements. As Trump has said: "Trade wars are good, and easy to win."

How can sovereignty and interdependence be reconciled? In the 19th century many progressives believed that the national principle was being superseded by the extraordinary advance of the world market and the interdependence it was creating in its wake. Marx and Engels spoke for most socialists when they wrote in the Communist Manifesto that: "The workers have no country. We cannot take from them what they have not got." This was one of their forecasts which did not turn out so well. The rise of nationalism as a political force and the binding of citizens into national communities was one of the most important political developments of the second half of the 19th century. Social democratic movements were obliged to develop on national lines but in their outlook they were resolutely internationalist, believing that the fight for democracy and social justice would only be fully won when peaceful cooperation between all peoples was achieved. Liberals too looked forward to the bonds of international commerce becoming stronger than territorial loyalties, allowing war to be gradually eliminated as an instrument of policy, giving way to a reign of peace and prosperity.

The growth of great power rivalry and nationalist politics led to the carnage of the first half of the 20th century. The liberal world order of the 19th century collapsed, and an era of national protectionism replaced it. The hopes of international cooperation proclaimed by Woodrow Wilson at Versailles after the first world war were dashed. The League of Nations proved a failure. One consequence was that progressives were forced to think much more in national terms, since the prospects of international cooperation seemed for a time so distant. After 1945 a liberal international order re-emerged under US leadership, designed to protect and support nation states and allowed them considerable freedom to determine their own domestic priorities. The emphasis was on building strong and resilient national democracies, which could command the legitimacy of their citizens, after the ravages of the previous three decades. When this system broke down and had to be reconfigured in the 1970s and 1980s, nation states kept their central place but had to adjust to new realities.

THE GLOBALISATION PARADOX

During the globalisation era growth rates were lower in the western democracies than they had been during the long boom of the 1950s and 1960s, but still substantial, and the most important aspect of this new period of prosperity was the rapid growth in Asia, particularly in the world's two most populous nations, India and China. But globalisation has created a paradox, of a kind familiar from the history of economic development. The economist Dani Rodrik has argued that states are forced to choose between global integration of economic trade and production, national sovereignty and national democracy. Any two can be combined but not all three.

What happened in the globalisation era up to the financial crash was that the first two – economic interdependence and national sovereignty – were secured at the expense of national democracy. For populist nationalists this became the discourse that governments had given away national sovereignty to external bodies like the EU. But national elites continued to exercise national sovereignty. They just became less accountable to their citizens as they learned to manage an increasingly complex, transnational international system through global networks and multilateral institutions. Since the financial crash this has begun to unravel because the plunge into austerity and the long-term stagnation of living standards and high unemployment rates of the young have fueled a democratic backlash. This is most evident in the increasing strength of the populist nationalists who have crowded on to the electoral stage, wanting to repudiate the way the elites have managed globalisation and condemn the way they have profited from it. They want to use the powers of the nation state to take back control, breaking up the networks of global elites, and re-establishing the accountability of national elites to their citizens.

The populist nationalist movement, as Steve Bannon has called it, is not confined to one nation. Its scope is international and the parties recognise one another as fighting a common fight. Their core beliefs are nationalist. They give priority to national sovereignty and its attributes – the control of borders, currency and laws. Populism for them is a tactical discourse, the counterposing of a virtuous, homogenous and unified people against corrupt, self-serving, anti-national global cosmopolitan elites. These parties have had some successes, but also some setbacks. They are far from winning everywhere, but they are in the ascendancy, and the defenders of the liberal international order are on the defensive. Globalisation is still moving forward. It has not yet gone into reverse, but the more national populists win, the more restricted international trade, migration and cultural exchange are likely to become. The flows of people, money, trade and services will all slow. Once a zero-sum logic takes hold it is hard to stop, because the rational course of action is to follow it through.

Many progressives lament that they do not want either of these two combinations – neither economic interdependence and national sovereignty which ignores democracy, nor national sovereignty and democracy which trashes economic interdependence. They would prefer to combine democracy with economic interdependence. But

that would require some kind of world government, or at least institutions which would make global elites accountable to the peoples
of the world. It may still be useful as a thought-experiment but the
practical obstacles to achieving it are so great just now as to put it
beyond reach.

But that leaves progressives adrift; unhappy with both alternatives
on offer yet by inclination more disposed to accept the first. In doing
so centre-left parties have been castigated for becoming agents of
the global elites, and therefore globalists, indistinguishable from
their centre-right rivals. Both supposedly promote greater economic
interdependence through the cooperation of national elites. In a
period of austerity that has been very damaging, and it is one of the
reasons why support for many centre-left parties has significantly
declined.

Are there ways out of this? The basic starting point has to be
acceptance of the nature of the dilemma. It cannot be wished away.
It is deeply embedded in the structure of the international system.
An Open Left has to have policies to deal with both sides of the
dilemma. It has to restate its commitment to a multilateral, rules-
based international order. Over the last 70 years (and even more so
in the last 30) this has become a cornerstone of progressive thinking.
There are some principled people on the left who profess internationalism but are against participation in any rules-based order, whether
it is the EU or the WTO, on the grounds that such participation limits
national sovereignty and constrains the ability of a democratically
elected government to pursue the policies it thinks appropriate for
its economy and society. This was a majority position in the British
Labour movement at the time of the first referendum on the UK's
membership of the European Economic Community in 1975, and it
also lay behind the 1983 manifesto which committed the party, not-
withstanding the referendum result eight years earlier, to withdraw
from the European Community.

Few on the progressive left share that view today. The big push
forward towards greater economic interdependence convinced many
former critics that the national protectionist era had closed, and that

any viable national economic policy had to take into account the realities of economic interdependence. It is no longer possible to consider the national economy in isolation. There have to be policies for not only the national level but also the regional and global levels. Forging trade agreements through treaties between sovereign states involves pooling sovereignty by agreeing to be bound by the rules set out in the treaty. Participation in all international agreements, from climate change to military alliances, is similar. Reflecting the degree of economic interdependence which has been achieved, a vast network of agencies and institutions have emerged to facilitate exchanges and cooperation in many different fields. Many national policies now need international partners and international agreements to be effective. States must extend their reach and capacity by cooperating with others.

The extent of interdependence should not be exaggerated. In many fields cooperation is still patchy and hard to organise. The failings of international cooperation are constantly being highlighted. But the sheer number of international organisations which now exist compared with 100 years ago shows that a qualitative change has taken place. At both global and regional levels states are enmeshed in a complex web of relationships, which make sharp distinctions between states as independent sovereign actors and the international market order harder to sustain. But, as the revival of protectionist rhetoric and measures shows, the tension between the two is still real and can burst into fresh life. One of the mistakes supporters of the western international order make is to suppose that it is permanent. Like all political constructions it is fragile and could be destroyed.

REGIONAL COOPERATION: THE CASE OF THE EUROPEAN UNION

The EU has been one of the most important examples of a multilateral order which has fostered cooperation between states through a combination of intergovernmental and supranational institutions.

It is the most developed of all the regionalist projects that have emerged around the world. Starting from small beginnings in the 1950s with just six members, it has grown to include 28 members (although with one, the UK, about to exit), and has in successive stages deepened its economic and political integration. But the basic character of the association, as an intergovernmental association with some supranational elements to uphold the treaties and develop their implications, has remained intact. Throughout its 60-year history, the EU has been an experiment in pooling sovereignty and developing common policies which are binding on all members.

The achievements of the EU have been impressive, but it has some serious shortcomings. Chief among these is its democratic deficit. The way the EU was established made this almost inevitable. It was set up and has been advanced through treaties between sovereign states. One of the many ironies of the Brexit debate was that because the EU adopted an intergovernmental approach, sacrificing democracy for the sake of national sovereignty, the resulting democratic deficit has been a rallying call for those calling for a reassertion of national sovereignty. Although a European parliament was established with direct elections to it, it was only granted limited powers. There is no European demos to which the main institutions of the EU – the council of ministers, the commission and the court of justice – are accountable. Therefore it often appears that there is no easy way for citizens to change the course of EU policy and the policymaking process is often cumbersome and opaque. It is understood very well by the elites which engage with it, but not at all well by citizens.

The disconnect between the European elites and the citizens mattered less when the union was expanding and the economy was doing well, but it has come to matter a great deal since the economic downturn and the imposition of austerity. There has also been limited progress in making EU symbols resonate with European citizens. A European identity is real for many Europeans but so far it has been less important for most of them than their national identities. Because the structures of accountability are weak popular legitimacy has been weak, and in recent years has been seriously eroded. This is also because the EU as an organisation tends to be focused inward on making intergovernmental cooperation and the pooling of sovereignty work. There is a lack of governing capacity, shown most clearly in the very low budget. It is only 1% of EU GDP. The budgets of member states are typically 40–55% of GDP, while the federal budget of the US is around 20% of US GDP. The EU makes ambitious claims for what it can do for citizens, but it often lacks the capacity or will to carry through. Citizens as a result often feel let down, and believe that the EU is either indifferent to their needs or unable to help. This has been felt acutely in recent years in Greece over the handling of its debt problem, and in Italy over the EU handling of immigration. At the heart of the problem is that the EU sometimes claims too much. It acts as though it were a state, but it is not a state; at most it is a confederation of states. Some want to see the EU emerge as a state, but so far the member states themselves, operating through the council of ministers, have always put the brakes on any push towards a strong form of federalism.

Most observers around the world view with amazement and not a little puzzlement Britain's decision to leave the EU, because from the outside membership of the EU has greatly increased the security and the prosperity of the countries that have joined. For progressives in the UK, most of whom supported remain in the referendum, the decision to leave makes maintaining Britain's security in the world more difficult. The costs of Brexit will be considerable, not just in economic terms, but also in terms of the UK's standing in the world and its ability to influence world events. Keeping the same level of cooperation that it currently has with its neighbours in a large number of fields will be immensely difficult, and the signal to the rest of the world that Britain is disengaging from multilateral cooperation and is choosing to become more isolated will be hard to overcome.

Those who back the strategy of a 'global Britain' are convinced that leave voters can be casually betrayed, and that a deregulated, low-wage, low-cost offshore tax haven is a viable future. It looks like a hard sell to the British electorate, and the much more likely prospect is that Britain, which was always a semi-detached member of the union, will opt in practice for an associate membership with the EU, which will align British regulation and standards in most areas very closely with the EU. As the full costs of exclusion from the single market become apparent, future UK governments may well seek to negotiate an even closer association. Brexit is a process rather than an event. In this way the damage may be limited, although leavers will complain that the result is BRINO, Brexit in name only.

For an Open Left, exclusion from Europe is a major setback, but without a sea change in the attitudes of leave voters, of which there is little sign, it is unlikely to be reversed in the short term. The task must therefore be to minimise the damage, and seek to maintain links and cooperation to as great an extent as possible. A global Britain that is not committed to multilateralism will not be a global Britain at all.

When Britain finally leaves the EU on 29 March 2019 this will not the end of the story. Like Norway, Britain will forever be debating what its relationship with 'Europe' should be. Should it move closer, should it move further away? Should it perhaps, after a decent interval, seek to rejoin, admitting that the costs of being excluded were too high, and that the benefits of 'independence' largely illusory? What is certain is that one vote in June 2016 has not settled the European issue in British politics. It has simply made it much more intractable and even more divisive.

IMMIGRATION

Immigration is one of the key challenges facing the EU and all the western democracies. It was a major factor in the Brexit vote. Although many of the leaders of the leave campaign held liberal views on immigration, that was not the case for a majority of leave voters, whose views were best represented by Nigel Farage and Ukip. Leave voters wanted Brexit to deliver a big reduction in the number of immigrants entering Britain (Farage suggested no more than 30,000 a year, down from 300,000, only half of whom were from the EU under free movement rules) (Figure 2.1). Many also wanted to send back a large proportion of the immigrants already in the UK, wherever they were from. Similar demands have been made by nationalist parties across Europe, in France, the Netherlands, Austria, Germany and Italy. Anti-Muslim feeling was an aspect of the Brexit vote as it has been in elections in many other European countries. The large numbers of economic migrants and asylum seekers attempting to enter the EU, and the inability so far of the EU to stem the flow or convince citizens that it is dealing effectively with the problem, have boosted support for populist nationalists.

The ability to control borders and determine who comes in and goes out is a key aspect of modern sovereignty. The idea of national self-determination has been an important progressive principle, implying the breakup of empires and large multinational states, which contained many national groupings held against their will. The idea that national identity should form the basis for political legitimacy was novel, but one which has become almost universal, enshrined in the charter of the UN, and still the cause of many conflicts throughout the world, as at present in Spain over Catalonia, wherever the aspiration to statehood is denied to a group which defines itself as a nation.

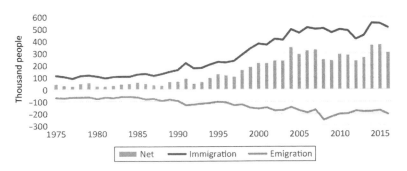

Figure 2.1   UK international migration (non-British citizens), 1975–2016. *Source*: ONS, Long-term International Migration 2.00, Citizenship, UK, 1975–2016.

Yet although the principle has been progressive, it also has a destructive side, shown in the rise of authoritarian and populist nationalisms and the use of the principle of national sovereignty by national elites to block international cooperation and agreement. In response some progressives have been tempted by the idea of open borders. Passports are a relatively recent innovation, introduced primarily to give governments more control over their populations. The Schengen agreement in 1985 did away with internal borders for a few countries and it has since been extended to most of the members of the EU. It has helped promote the free flow of citizens, trade, tourism and cultural exchange. The ending of hard borders in the EU has helped solve long-standing problems, such as the status of South Tyrol, which was handed to Italy after the first world war, yet whose population still wanted to affirm their identity with the rest of the Tyrol which was part of Austria. Once Austria joined the EU all borders were dismantled, and the rights of South Tyroleans to express their identity, language and culture were guaranteed, while formal sovereignty remained with Italy. Similarly a key part of the Good Friday Agreement, which brought peace to Northern Ireland after three decades of terrorist violence, was the status of the border between Northern Ireland and the Republic. It was dismantled, allowing free movement of goods and people across it. One of the costs of Brexit is that it threatens to unravel that settlement by requiring a border to be reimposed.

It is easy to point to the harm caused by closed borders, but open borders also have their downsides. One such problem is the encouragement they give to the free movement of capital as well as people and goods, and the effect which that can have on housing markets, particularly in capital cities like London. But an even bigger downside of open borders is economic migration and the effect this can have on established communities and neighbourhoods. This issue is partly about competition for resources – jobs, housing, public services – and partly about cultural identity, and perceived threats to it. The rate of migration is crucial, because it determines how easily migrants can integrate with local communities. Some on the left argue there should be no controls on immigration at all, but that seems impossible to sustain politically. Events in many European countries, Italy being the latest example, show how toxic an issue very high levels of economic migration have become, and the backlash they are causing, leading to the rise of virulently anti-immigrant and racist parties.

An Open Left recognises that there are tradeoffs in this area as in any other. It is one of the hardest issues that progressives have to confront. Increasing levels of economic migration have many causes, which include the effects of civil wars and famines. The displacement of peoples has long been characteristic of the modern era. But the primary causes are the desire of migrants to better themselves and shortages of labour in the rich countries. At times immigration has been positively welcomed, as in the US in the 19th century when immigrants were needed to populate the new territories which were springing up behind an ever-expanding frontier, as the Native Americans were evicted from their lands. Such times do not, though, last indefinitely because land and resources are never unlimited.

Progressives naturally and rightly resist the stigmatising and scapegoating of immigrants and asylum seekers, which nationalist media encourage through selective anecdotes and the stoking of fears and anxieties. However, they also have to find ways to reassure and protect those communities most affected. Local communities have to be involved in the decisions to accept more immigrants. If they are not welcoming they will become resentful, feeling that immigration is something over which they have no control.

The problem is particularly hard to tackle because of the tension between economic interdependence and national sovereignty. The principle of free movement for all citizens within each national jurisdiction has been widely if not universally accepted. The right to move around for work, residence and study have become recognised as key aspects of democratic citizenship. The apartheid system in South Africa was an example of what happens when that right is denied. But it has proved much harder to extend this principle outside the borders of nation states. The EU is one of the few examples where this has been realised, through the principle of free movement embedded in the rules of the single market. Elsewhere, though, the fragmentation of the world into national jurisdictions has made the distinctions between insiders and outsiders and friends and enemies key dividing lines in the construction of the tribal politics of nationalism.

The challenge for an Open Left is how to maintain a commitment to an open, multilateral international order while at the same maintaining a liberal order within a sovereign state. An Open Left has to be committed to equality of all citizens within a state, but what then is the obligation to those outside the state? The willingness of politicians in the rich western democracies to support the rules of a liberal international order often stops when it comes to migration. Politicians in the rich countries are expected to preserve and protect the privileges which have accrued over a long period of time to the populations of the rich countries. The free movement of labour across the whole world is resisted because it threatens the rents which all the citizens of the rich countries enjoy from three centuries of western dominance of the world. This is one of the hardest obstacles to the creation of a non-western-centric international order. One of the paradoxes of the situation is that since 1945 quite high levels of immigration have become necessary for western economies to function. Flexible labour markets have become a key factor in many economies seeking to boost their economic growth.

There are no easy ways out of the dilemmas this poses for policy. From a progressive standpoint, there is a trade-off to be made between the flexibility of labour markets and the rate of economic growth if that means that the impact of immigration on communities that feel left behind can be controlled and seen to be controlled. But often the areas with the highest antagonism towards immigrants are the ones with the lowest number of immigrants. These paradoxes have to be honestly confronted as a reality of our politics. It is therefore necessary both to get democratic consent to how liberal immigration policy should be, and to implement policies aimed at accelerating development in poor countries and transferring wealth from the rich countries to them directly. Without such measures the pressure of economic migrants to enter the rich countries will continue to grow.

FOREIGN POLICY AND DEFENCE

The basic aim of a progressive foreign policy is simple enough: to avoid wars and secure peace. The conflicts which have disfigured human history arising from civil wars, imperialist expansion and great power rivalries have been a central part of modernity and its tortuous evolution. As technology has advanced so the destructiveness of the weapons available has increased to the point where human beings have acquired the means to make themselves extinct.

Some of the early liberal optimism that war would die out as commerce expanded proved sadly premature. Economic interdependence advanced in an extraordinary fashion in the 19th century, but politics lagged far behind. The continuing fragmentation of political authority fuelled rivalries between the great powers and ensured that, when they did break out, conflicts were more wide-ranging and deadly than any that had previously occurred. The basic insight of liberal thinkers was not wrong however. The spread of commercial society, and the new technologies and means of communication it made possible, have created the basis for solidarity between peoples which has never existed before. It has created common experiences, common values and common standards. These are all essential foundations on which a more peaceful world can be built, and since 1945 has been built.

But the peace we have is fragile. Not only are there many small wars and civil wars, but the shadow of nuclear extermination still hangs over the world. The problem of nuclear proliferation has not been solved, and since the end of the cold war more countries have acquired nuclear weapons. The two former superpowers have substantially reduced their nuclear arsenals, decommissioning many weapons, but very large nuclear arsenals still exist. The political task is to continue the painstaking attempts to construct an international order which can constrain powerful states, and create institutions for resolving differences and conflicts. In a world of fragmented jurisdictions this often seems an impossible and fruitless task, and the many reverses, defeats and disappointments create despondency about whether there can ever be any lasting progress.

The problem is starkly visible in the development of international law. The establishment of a rule of law for the international order, as well as for individual countries, is obviously desirable. But there is a crucial difference. The rule of law, in the sense of due process and independent courts, requires the state to be organised in a particular way. There has to be a culture which accepts the rule of law and the constitutional rules and conventions which uphold it. All the different branches of the state – particularly the executive, legislature, civil service and military – have to accept their subordination to the rule of law and be bound by it. In all democracies the rule of law is tested from time to time, and occasionally subverted, but then there is usually a reaction and it is reasserted. Laws can, of course, be changed, but only in ways that are themselves part of the rule of law. A country in which any part of the state starts flouting the rule of law with impunity soon ceases to be considered a democracy. Law becomes an instrument in the hands of the ruling elite.

In the international system none of this applies, because there is no single constituted authority which can uphold the rule of law and enforce the judgements of international courts. Rulings can only be enforced through intergovernmental cooperation. The international criminal court at the Hague shows that very clearly. Many powerful states, including the US, do not recognise the court and refuse to be bound by it. The trials it is able to conduct are generally of individuals who have lost the protection of their states. We are still at an early stage in the development of a rule of law which could apply universally. What we have at the moment are some oases of the rule of law, but many states who do not uphold the rule of law within their own jurisdictions, or, if they do, are not willing to subordinate themselves to a higher court. The EU is a remarkable experiment in creating a rule of law which covers all its members and is upheld through the European court of justice (ECJ). Its basis is the agreement of its members to pool their sovereignty through a set of intergovernmental treaties. This has worked because all the member states are democracies which uphold the rule of law in their own jurisdictions. Even so it is a source of populist and nationalist discontent, and being subject to rulings of the ECJ rather than the British courts was one of the main issues on which the campaign to leave the EU was based.

International law is precarious because there is no political authority to uphold and implement its rulings. There is also a problem of interpreting what the law is, since there is no international court of justice comparable to the ECJ. One authoritative source should be the UN security council, but this is a political body and the five permanent members have vetoes, so can block any ruling they judge to be against their interest. Only three of the five permanent members are full democracies and apply the rule of law in their own jurisdictions. The ability of powerful states to pursue their own interests, relying on their own interpretation of international law, was demonstrated in the case of the US invasion of Iraq in 2003 and Russia's annexation of Crimea in 2014 and its interventions in Ukraine and Georgia. Such violations are inherent in the way the international state system is organised. The most powerful states will still intervene when it is in their interests to do. What has become much less common in the last 70 years has been states pursuing territorial aggrandisement against their neighbours. There are still many territorial disputes but mostly of a lesser kind and more amenable to resolution than many of the disputes in the past.

One of the reasons for this has been the existence of the UN. It is widely dismissed as ineffective in resolving conflicts once they have broken out. The civil war in Syria is often cited as another example of UN failure. But the UN is not a sovereign body and its capacities and resources are only those which its member states, and particularly its most powerful member states, agree to let it have.

What the UN has succeeded in doing is to establish a framework of norms and rules for international relations which have helped develop international law, and has slowly changed perceptions of what is legitimate and what not. Enshrined in the UN charter is the principle of national self-determination, and the rule that each properly constituted state should not suffer interference from other states in its internal affairs. After centuries of colonial expansion and wars of territorial aggrandisement, this affirmed a key progressive principle. It was carefully hedged with conditions outlining when it might be appropriate for one state to use force against another. Self-defence has always been the most important category. The US attack on Afghanistan in 2001 was judged by the UN security council to be an act of self-defence following the 9/11 terrorist attack by al-Qaida on the US. Other grounds for disregarding the rule banning the use of force by one state against another to resolve disputes are vaguer, but have become increasingly important. Does the international community have a responsibility to protect citizens of a particular territory, if, for example, their government is conducting genocide, inflicting famine or in other ways oppressing part of its people, and denying them their human rights? These rights are also guaranteed under the UN charter.

Doctrines of liberal internationalism have lost most of their advocates since the Iraq war. It has become easy to forget that some interventions justified by the responsibility to protect have been broadly successful. Sierra Leone and Kosovo were two such in which Britain was involved. Any intervention will always be controversial, though, and has to be judged by clear and precise criteria. As Britain's foreign secretary, Robin Cook supported the interventions in Sierra Leone and Kosovo but he did not support the invasion of Iraq and resigned from the government as a result. His resignation statement makes a powerful case for intervention only when the evidence is overwhelming and a number of clear tests have been met. As he put it, the bar for intervention has to be especially high, and in his judgement fell short in the case of Iraq. The war was popular at the time. When Basra and Baghdad fell early on in the conflict more than 60% of Britons supported the war. Then opinion soured, because of the failure to find weapons of mass destruction, the main justification for the war, and the difficulties of the occupation and the mounting number of British and Iraqi casualties. Public opinion turned against the Iraq war and against all interventions in which British lives might be placed at risk. It has become difficult to imagine the circumstances in which British ground forces may again be committed to a foreign war. Britain still has a significant military capacity but it is unlikely to make much use of it. In this it has come to resemble other European states.

This relates to another point. An Open Left supports not only the principle of self-defence but strong defence capabilities. Britain has gone from being a country which devoted 8% of its national income to defence in the years after 1945 to one which now spends less than 2% on defence. As long as there are dictatorships and closed societies, such expenditure will remain necessary. For some time, the UK has been a middle-ranking power but it still retains a permanent seat on the UN security council. Its right to that seat, especially after Brexit, will depend on how willing the UK is to stay engaged with the rest of the world; to continue to fund an extensive diplomatic network; to commit its military to help with UN peacekeeping and the enforcement of international law; and to maintain its commendable commitment to a high level of foreign aid, despite strong opposition from the populist nationalist media. An effective defence needs constant review of defence commitments and the best way to meet them. Britain's deep-seated attachment to its independent nuclear deterrent, which – as Enoch Powell once remarked – is neither independent nor a deterrent, has become a barrier to rational defence planning and deciding whether the money devoted to Trident might not be better spent on other capabilities.

It also has to be a priority of any progressive foreign policy to support in all possible ways the establishment of more stable democracies around the world, reversing the tendency recently for the number to decline. Ever since Kant argued for the creation of a league of republics it has been an axiom of progressive thinking about international relations that peace and stability are likely to be enhanced the more states embrace the rule of law and republican and democratic principles. Cooperation between such states is easier, and there are more internal restraints on their behaviour. They are more likely to support multilateral institutions and pragmatic compromises when conflicts of interest arise. The EU has been a contemporary version of the leagues of republics. Although it has suffered blows in recent times with the decision of the UK to give up its membership, the authoritarian direction taken by some of its newer members, and the populist insurgency against many of the EU's core values, the EU remains a champion of liberal and democratic values and the most developed experiment in multilateral cooperation between sovereign nation states.

The postwar international order owed its success and its durability to the fact that during the cold war its core alliances, such as Nato and the EU, were leagues of democracies. The challenge in creating a non-western-centric international order is that many of the players that need to be involved are not democracies at all, or are at best illiberal democracies. It is still vital to attempt to construct governance arrangements and a set of common rules and norms which as many countries as possible will sign up to. The 2015 Paris climate change agreement showed what is possible. The institutional focus of a new international order might initially be the G20. Even though it still excludes most states in the world, it would be a big step forward. The G20 was given added prominence for a time after the 2008 financial crash but has since faded. Reviving it should be a priority for progressive statecraft. Existing international bodies, like the IMF, the World Bank, the WTO and the Financial Stability Board, could then be restructured to reflect the changing importance of countries in the global economy. The G20 should be invited to endorse an updated version of the UN Millennium Development Goals as a basic statement of aims for the new international order, with participation from global civil society organisations.

We are a long way from realising such an international order. But it should be a crucial aim for an Open Left to do whatever it can to bring it about. The various leagues of western democracies, above all the EU, are essential building blocks for this new world order, and need wherever possible to be further strengthened, but it can no longer just be confined to them. It has to go wider, and spaces for continual dialogue and negotiation created. The more inclusive these can be made to be, the more durable will be the order that can be created. But there will always be tradeoffs.

Our understanding of what security means in an increasingly interdependent and connected world is changing. New notions of human security have widened the meaning of security from being concerned primarily with the defence of a state from other states, to a focus on the main global forces and trends that threaten the wellbeing of citizens, and which states must try and guard against. These include threats from non-state actors such as international criminals, particularly the networks promoting drug smuggling and money laundering, and international terrorism, as well as threats arising from wider risks, including environmental dangers, global poverty, water and food shortages, and global pandemics. An Open Left favours international cooperation and multilateral agreements to help tackle these problems. Britain can contribute specialist defence forces and intelligence services to these endeavours, and it is vital that it should do so. In the aftermath of Brexit Britain will have to work harder to prove that it wants to stay engaged. Maintaining strong cooperation between the UK and the EU on security and defence will be more difficult, but it will be a key goal for a progressive foreign policy.

ECONOMY

At the heart of any progressive project is political economy, an understanding of how wealth is created and distributed and how institutions might be reformed and behaviour changed to achieve progressive goals. As the name suggests, political economy is about the interaction of politics and economics, and about how stubborn political and economic realities put constraints on what is possible and achievable. But within every political economy there is also a moral economy, which is concerned with what is desirable rather than with what exists, and this inspires different visions of how economy and society might be organised to maximise the wellbeing of its members.

We need a new moral economy today to inspire a transformative political economy and to guide the emergence of a new economic model. The failings of our existing economic model were highlighted by the 2008 crash. Our present model of political economy has become unbalanced between global markets and local economies, global cities and small towns, shareholder value and stakeholder value, and global corporations and domestic households. We need to find new ways of making progressive values compatible with market efficiency; achieving a dynamic, entrepreneurial, innovating and more decentralised economy; and promoting a sharing economy, mutualism and ethical practice, and new forms of local finance such as crowdfunding. This chapter explores some of the ideas on the progressive left about how to rethink the nature of our economy and put human wellbeing and the perseveration of our natural environment at the centre of economic policy.

The political economy of the progressive left has been shaped by three main strategies in the last 100 years. The first was the planned economy, which sought to suppress or replace markets by the application of direct controls and the ownership of productive assets to the state. This strategy rested on the belief that markets were inherently inefficient and wasteful, rested on exploitation and produced inequality, thus destroying communities and making the poor and least equipped members of society pay the costs of economic progress. The enthusiasm for planning was not confined to the left. It was also championed in different ways by the right. There was a reaction to the free-market capitalism of the 19th century and its failure to provide the kind of security and stability considered necessary for political legitimacy and industrial advance. Industrial societies needed a much more extended state to provide services which could not be provided by the market. Socialists wanted a fully planned economy to replace capitalism. They disagreed over how quickly this might be achieved, and whether a political and social revolution was needed. But with few dissenters most progressives came to place their faith in the use of state power to transform the economy. Planning was regarded as a method of coordination that was superior to the market. The expectation of those advancing it was that public ownership and central planning of labour, land, trade and finance would achieve a superior economic performance, more growth, higher productivity and therefore more resources to distribute to create a fairer society.

The second strategy, the Keynesian welfare state, was concerned less with replacing capitalism and markets with an alternative economic system than with setting limits to the way in which it operated. It sought to establish countervailing powers and institutions, a framework of rules which sought to control and channel the forces which capitalism unleashed. It set out to protect those sectors of the economy which were not commodified and to extend them into areas that were. The aim was to create a parallel economy which was not subject to market exchange but financed from taxation by the state, and under its direct control. The expansion of welfare programmes, in particular universal benefits and universal provision in health and education, Keynesian demand management, aimed to create full employment and smooth out the capitalist business cycle, and public ownership of the main utilities became the key elements of this strategy. This enlarged public sector existed alongside the private sector, and could be conceived as complementary to it, but was also antagonistic to it since its ethos and method of coordination and finance were so different. The aim of this strategy was to tame the market by eliminating its excesses, and to counter the way market forces left unchecked systematically created inequality and insecurity. Rather than the complete replacement of capitalism it advocated the creation of a more pluralist and balanced economy, in which different principles of political economy would be recognised as being appropriate in different spheres.

The third strategy was a response both to setbacks in delivering a planned economy, which could raise economic growth, and a welfare state which could abolish poverty, as well as to the rise of aggressive pro-market ideologies and programmes that sought to shift the priorities in economic policy from planning and welfare to markets and competition. The strategy of the third way tried to overcome the traditional dichotomy between states and markets in social democratic thinking and practice. Markets were recognised as the primary institutional mechanism for ensuring dynamism and innovation in the economy, with states playing an enabling role, steering the economy rather than trying to directly control it, and regulating markets rather than seeking to replace or suppress them. The goal was to combine economic efficiency and social justice. If the market economy could be made more successful by smart government policies, there would be more resources through the tax system to expand the provision of welfare, health and education.

What was novel about this third way thinking for many socialists and social democrats was that it showed that progressives did not need to fight markets, they could work with them, using markets as tools to realise their goals. Collectivist social democracy had united social justice and economic efficiency through planning and the imposition of a rational plan from the centre. Welfare social democracy had tended to separate social justice and economic efficiency by making the first the preserve of the public sector and the second the preserve of the private sector. Third way social democracy sought to restore the unity, by giving priority to market mechanisms in both the public and private sectors, within a framework of the common good determined by the state.

At different historical points all three strategies enabled centre-left parties to win support from voters for transformative economic policies. But all in the end have had to be discarded. The third way policies which had seemed so successful at the turn of the century were discredited by the 2008 financial crash and its aftermath. Since then the centre left has seemed adrift, unable to resist effectively the imposition of austerity or to offer an alternative that resonates with voters. At such times it is necessary to go back to fundamentals and reconnect with the moral purpose of a progressive political economy, as well as reflecting on the constraints and opportunities which now face us.

As this brief sketch of the three historical strategies shows, the centre left has always tended to think that the key question in political economy is the relationship between states and markets. Markets come in many varieties – from transport and supermarkets, which are highly regulated, to car-boot sales, cyberspace, data companies and crypto-currencies, which currently operate with very little regulation at all. What is important about markets is that once they cease to be purely local and enough goods are traded on them, they are able to coordinate human economic activity on a vast scale. They do not do this spontaneously and naturally. They require active political and legal interventions to create the conditions in which they can function. Markets work when there is a strong rule of law, enforcement of contract and property rights, a stable form of money, enforcement of a degree of competition, public order and political stability, and a high degree of trust. Such trust tends to develop when all these other conditions are in place. Markets in this sense are rule-governed orders. The reason they work is that they are decentralised and impersonal, allowing the construction of elaborate and complex supply chains, connecting buyers and sellers across oceans and continents, and allowing an ever-deepening division of labour to take hold. Markets have therefore become an indispensable support for prosperity in the modern world. They can be suppressed and obstructed but only at the cost of a big reduction in wealth. The international trading system is hard to leave once states have become full participants within it. It is possible to exist outside the international trading system, as the Soviet Union largely did during the cold war, and as North Korea is trying to do today. However, the economic costs are high, and few societies once having tasted the benefits of an open market system are willing to give them up.

The centre left has traditionally positioned itself firmly as the defender of states against markets. But this is a very misleading way to think about political economy. It merely reverses the standard terms of liberal political economy, which see markets as natural, spontaneous and benign, and states as artificial, bureaucratic and oppressive. It has serious political consequences as well. By identifying with the state and the public sector, the centre left falls into a trap. In modern economies, where the great majority work in the private sector and there are more self-employed people than trade unionists, the centre left is easily dismissed as the party representing the interests of public sector workers and welfare benefit recipients, both minorities. In using the dichotomy between states and markets, and emotionally backing the former against the latter, the centre left confirms this perception. Since support for taking sectors of the economy into public ownership – beyond major public utilities like the railways and natural monopolies like water – is small, the centre left risks being seen as out of touch with the economy in which most people work.

A way to avoid this trap is to think more deeply about the distinctive form of political economy which characterises the modern world. One way to do this is to start not with markets and states, but with households. This is a perspective developed by feminist political economists such as Ruth Pearson, with her analysis of the reproductive economy, and also by political economists at the Centre for Research on Socio-Cultural Change, with their work on the foundational economy, and by the Labour MP Rachel Reeves in her call to focus on the 'everyday economy'. These different conceptions show that there is not one unified economy but several economies, which are related in complex ways. There is the globalised market economy, where goods and services are internationally traded and activity is driven by profit maximisation, competition and shareholder value; there is the local or foundational economy, the 'everyday economy', employing about one-third of the workforce, and comprising the production and distribution of food, the organisation of vital services like education and health, and public utilities such as transport, heat, water and light; there is the reproductive or household economy, which comprises the unpaid care activities necessary to secure the biological and everyday reproduction of human beings; and there is the green economy, which measures the impacts of human activities in all three of the other economies on the biosphere, such as our carbon footprint, use of natural resources and impact on biodiversity.

Economic activity and economy growth are traditionally assessed from the standpoint of the globalised market economy, as though this was the only one which was important, but this economy sustains itself by offloading costs on to the other three economies, as well as continually encroaching on them. We get a very different view of economic activity if we view it from the perspective of the local economy, the household economy or the green economy. It gives us very different measures of what counts as economic success and what the goals of economic activity should be. It provides a new moral economy to inform the policies of a progressive political economy, aimed at rebalancing the economy and restoring prosperity and security for citizens wherever they live and work, in global hubs, big cities, small town or rural villages.

A progressive economic programme needs policies for all four economies, and it needs to change the way we evaluate economic success. This would be a transformative political economy, which would establish a very different economic model and one which would have very different priorities. The directors of the Sheffield Political Economy Research Institute, Colin Hay and Tony Payne, have called it 'civic capitalism', others have spoken of the sharing economy or the green new deal. What is important in all of them is that the success or failure of economic activity is measured not as it is conventionally measured by indices of output and productivity, but by indices of human wellbeing. A sustainable economic index, for example, can track such things as inequality, changes in per capita energy use and changes in carbon emissions, while a reproductive index might focus on health, education, lifelong learning, skills upgrading and the quality of care services – the public goods that underpin a dignified life for everyone at every age.

At the root of this approach to political economy is the understanding that households are organised on very different lines from markets. Domestic households are the original *economies* in the Greek meaning of the word. They have a collective purpose and a directing will. They can be hierarchical or egalitarian. They are organised around sharing, planning, allocating and distributing, rather than exchanging. They balance their in-goings and out-goings, seeking to economise, reducing costs and expenditure to ensure that accounts balance. Households are intimately concerned with the welfare of their members and the fairness of how they distribute their resources and tasks. Markets could not exist without households, yet they are very different from them. Markets tend to be unplanned and decentralised while households tend to be planned and centralised. It is why many economic liberals dislike households. They are little bastions of socialism and collectivism, which can foster resistance to the impersonal rules and outcomes of the market.

If political economy is viewed from the perspective of the household, attention is focused on questions of the wellbeing and welfare of members of the household, and how they are affected by relationships within the household and relationships with other households and the world outside the household. What matters is the health and happiness of individuals and the opportunities and constraints, advantages and handicaps, which determine their life chances. The purpose of such a political economy becomes to enhance the quality of the lives people live. It is about the tangible, direct experiences of individuals, and their interactions with one another and with markets, companies and states. This perspective in political economy exposes the costs which are placed disproportionately on some members of households rather than others, particularly women. Without households markets could not function, nor could states, yet in our preoccupation with the big questions of markets and states we forget that the wellbeing of members of the household should be the criterion by which the success or failure of markets and state is judged.

When we think of households we think primarily of private domestic households, based on the family unit. But states are households and so are companies. They are much more complex than domestic households but their bureaucratic and hierarchical structures make them planned economies, and therefore households, rather than unplanned and impersonal markets. Therefore they operate outside the perfect rationality which economists' models assume. A progressive political economy has to be grounded on an appreciation of how markets and the different kinds of household interact. These are insights shared by several traditions in political economy including institutionalist economics in the 1930s and feminist political economy today.

The state as the public household has a special role in making markets possible and in regulating them, but to focus on the relationship between markets and the state, ignoring the role of domestic households and companies, is a big mistake. Market 'forces' are made up of the decisions of a multitude of households – domestic, corporate and public. Because they have no overall planning, market economies are dynamic and creative but also unstable, prone to cycles of activity and periodic crashes and slumps. Many households suffer as a result but the pain is not evenly spread. The way that capitalism has always worked is to socialise losses and privatise profits. States are crucial in ensuring this. They are the lenders of last resort, as demonstrated once again in the 2008 financial crash when the banks were bailed out. If the state had refused to act in this way the result would have been a catastrophic slump. But states not only socialise losses, they also privatise them by forcing households to bear some of the costs by cutting spending and lowering or withdrawing benefits. That makes the state look at times subordinate to major corporate players, but it also shows how they could not function without the state.

Two of the great conundrums of political economy are why is it so hard to reduce the size of the state and why is it so hard to regulate some markets, particularly financial markets? The answer is that the state as the public household has always provided essential public goods without which markets could not function, and in the course of the last 100 years, as industrial societies have become increasingly complex, the need for an extended state has grown. At the same time as there is a constant tendency for markets to reach beyond the territorial jurisdictions of states, companies have grown enormously in scale, reach and capacity. That makes them increasingly hard to regulate by even the largest states, since states come to rely on those companies for the achievement of so many of the things they need.

AFTER THE CRASH

The financial crash of 2008 changed our political economy in ways we do not yet fully understand. Ten years since the credit crunch began western economies are still not operating normally. Interest rates have been at historic lows all through this time and only began to lift off the floor in 2017. Quantitative easing has yet to be unwound. No one is certain what will happen when it is, since it has been responsible for keeping asset prices high for the last 10 years. Productivity remains low (Figure 3.1) and wages and living standards stagnant. Is the secular stagnation of the last decade the new normal, or the new mediocre, as Christine Lagarde has termed it? If so, there are serious implications for all governments, not just progressive ones. Every serious crisis is a crisis of beliefs, and that goes for critics of the status quo as well as its defenders. On the surface very little seems to have changed. The old mantras are still repeated. But underneath there is considerable disquiet. The crisis of 2008 is slowly forcing a fundamental rethinking of some of the core assumptions that have governed economic policy for the last 30 years. A number of influential commentators and regulators have begun to question things that were once taken for granted. Partly this is because many familiar policies have evidently failed or no longer work, but it is also in response to the new circumstances and challenges which the period since the crash has brought into sharp relief.

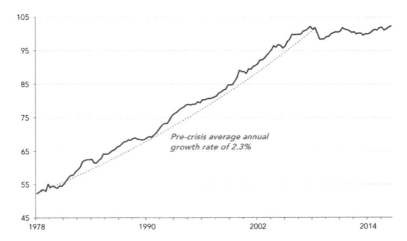

Figure 3.1 Productivity in the UK, 1978–2016 (2013=100). *Source*: Corlett, A and Clarke, S (2017) Living Standards, Resolution Foundation.

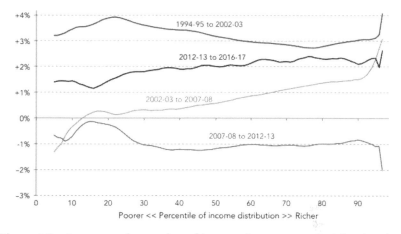

Figure 3.2 Average real annual working age income growth (after housing costs) in the UK, 1994/5–2016/17. *Source*: Corlett, A and Clarke, S (2017) Living Standards, Resolution Foundation.

The challenge which everyone hears about is how to return to economic growth. However, there are different kinds of growth and there are tradeoffs to make between them. In our political economy it is very hard to imagine a world in which there would be no growth, just sufficient activity to maintain the society and the capital stock at its present level. Many utopias have imagined it, however, and human-made climate change has begun to make it highly relevant, since some argue it is the only way we can avert a catastrophe later in this century. From time to time, political economists have advocated it and even predicted it, but politically it has always been put firmly in the too difficult box. Apart from some green politicians, no mainstream politicians are brave enough to campaign on it. Instead, all politicians promise to keep the economy growing and argue about how the proceeds of growth should be distributed. The demands for more funding for both private and public consumption appears insatiable and unstoppable.

One of the consequences of the steady incremental rise in living standards over the last 200 hundred years is that the expectation that growth is now linear and continuous instead of cyclical has become embedded. In societies where this kind of economic progress has taken hold every generation has come to expect to be better off than the previous one. Periods of economic difficulty and austerity when living standards stagnate or decline are also periods of political difficulty. This gives added weight to the lobby for growth. When recessions happen the task of policy is to take measures to allow a recovery to take place as soon as possible. Parties thought to offer the best chance of returning the economy quickly to prosperity and growth are rewarded with support.

In western democracies all the political focus is on how to achieve this return to growth. This is not a problem in China, India or Africa. There the potential for growth and the need for growth is still massive, with so many citizens still poor and on the land, and with room for policies of catch up with the world's developed economies. It is very different in the mature capitalist economies of North America, Europe and Japan. Recessions and slumps historically have been short-lived, even in the 1930s. Since 1945 they have lasted on average 18 months, before a full recovery was under way. The slow recovery since the crash has been unprecedented and perplexing. Something else is obviously going on but what, and what can be done about it? Bearing in mind the environmental risks we are running, should anything be done about it?

Opinion is very divided on what was the appropriate response to the crash. One argument is that it should have been allowed to run its course. The banks should not have been bailed out. A massive wave of bankruptcies would have marked down the value of all assets to the point where the economy would have rebounded into positive growth, free of the vast debts – public, private and corporate – accumulated during the boom. This was the medicine applied after 1929. The soaring levels of unemployment, poverty and distress led to political upheavals, which included the rise of the Nazis in Germany. Strong medicine can sometimes kill as well as cure. No progressive party could have supported such a drastic policy.

A second argument, which has prevailed up to now almost everywhere, is that after the financial shock and the recession the priority had to be returning to the status quo as quickly as possible. This meant zero interest rates reinforced by quantitative easing to preserve the financial liquidity of the banks by keeping up asset prices, and austerity policies applied to public services to shrink the size of the state to the reduced size of the economy, adding to deflationary pressure. The theory was that the quicker the deficit could be eliminated by austerity measures the quicker the recovery would come. This became known as the doctrine of expansionary austerity. It failed. Instead, these policies kept economies afloat but stagnant, the recovery weak, and living standards for the majority stagnant or falling. Most political effort was put into reducing the deficit in the public finances, ignoring the accumulation of debt elsewhere, as well as the financial surpluses in the corporate sector in which companies were reluctant to invest, seeing no profitable investment opportunities. One consequence was the steady build-up of resentment against the financial and corporate elites and their supporters in the political class, who were regarded as being unfairly protected at the expense of the rest of the community.

A third argument, advanced by many on the progressive left, is that the authorities were right to do what they did, saving the financial system and averting a complete financial collapse, but then they should have initiated a radical reconstruction of the failed policies and institutions of the previous era. Austerity was unavoidable in the sense that a plan was needed to eliminate the deficit on current spending, but progressive governments would have asked, austerity for whom? Burdens would have been distributed very differently, with the balance being achieved through higher taxation rather than spending cuts. Households would have been protected rather than bankers and asset holders.

Instead of preparing for a return to business as usual as soon as possible, progressive governments would have been much more determined to break with that approach by rebalancing the economy, reorganising finance, and launching a major investment programme in the household and local economies, focusing on affordable housing, social care, infrastructure, skills, research and innovation. This would have meant accepting that, despite record low interest rates, such investment would not come from the private sector but only from the public. Although debt and borrowing would have been higher, a sounder long-term platform for prosperity, wellbeing and social cohesion might have been secured. This would have been a Keynesian plus strategy, breaking from the discredited inflation targeting of the previous economic model, and seeing the role of the state as to provide the conditions in which all parts of the economy could move forward again.

These three prescriptions differed markedly in their diagnosis and remedies but share in common the belief that the financial crash and the recession were temporary shocks, and that a way can be found to restore western economies to the path of steady annual growth, rising prosperity and renewed political legitimacy and social cohesion. Against that optimism others argue that the western economies are hovering on the edge of a deflation trap and are mired in long-term secular stagnation, which they do not know how to break out of. This is seen as politically dangerous because it increases support for populist nationalists like Trump, whose policies threaten to tear down the edifice of western prosperity erected so painstakingly over 70 years. Some of the evidence for this view is compelling. The economist Robert Gordon and others have argued that western economies have reached a technological frontier. The low-hanging fruit has all been picked and, although we live in a time of ever-accelerating and breathless technological innovation, the actual pay-off of these innovations – raising productivity and having a generalisable wealth effect across the whole economy – has so far been much less than comparable universal technologies of the past, such as the steam engine or electricity. Profitable investment opportunities on the scale needed to improve productivity have proved insufficient. The ability to outsource production using very cheap labour in Asia has added to the relative unattractiveness of investment. The flexibility of labour markets particularly in the UK and the US was supposed to offset that, but its main effect has been to create many low-paid, temporary and precarious jobs in the service economy.

Western economies appear stuck in a long stagnation of productivity and living standards, overturning the assumptions about normal growth and prosperity which has been a hardcore assumption of mainstream political economy for most of the postwar period. If this was really so it would be a major break with the past. The counter-argument is that it is still too early to be sure what is happening to the economy and what the ultimate impact of information technology and the digital revolution is likely to be. The optimists agree that so far some of the main innovations have been the platforms developed by internet companies like Facebook, Google and Amazon, but argue that the real benefits of the information revolution are only just starting to appear. They point to the potential for replacing huge numbers of jobs in manufacturing, retail and services, including professional services. The second machine age, the rise of artificial intelligence, will potentially bring a dramatic increase in productivity comparable to previous revolutions, as labour is released from traditional employments. New industries and services, and new forms of employment and self-employment, will spring up to mop up those displaced. In this way the whole economy advances and generates more wealth.

Which of these views of the future economy is more nearly right matters a lot for a progressive political economy. It may come down to timing. The evidence of the slow recovery and the secular stagnation of output and living standards is clear enough. It has defined the last 10 years. But how much longer will it last? The economic revival in some countries, particularly the US and those in the eurozone in 2017 and 2018, raised hopes that a more lasting recovery might finally be under way, with productivity, investment and wages all increasing, allowing interest rates finally to rise. There remain huge risks around this process, and fears that it could be another short-lived boom, and that the economy will again relapse. Worse still is the danger that the recklessness of US policy under Trump in cutting taxes and increasing spending simultaneously while threatening trade wars could trigger another financial collapse, and this time, as the HSBC bank has warned, there are no lifeboats left.

What is undeniable is the enormous potential of the new information economy, which is clearly only in its early stages. Some of its applications like 3D printing could revolutionise production and change the way economies operate, undercutting many existing forms of comparative advantage. It is likely at some stage that the optimists will be proved right. The conditions for a big new advance in prosperity and growth are building. However, some of the other conditions for a new boom are not yet in place and too many of the reasons for the collapse of the last one have not been dealt with. This is the opening for a progressive political economy. There needs to be a plan to unlock the potential of the new technologies by removing some of the obstacles which currently exist. Those drawing up the plan must also think hard about the policies which will be needed to redistribute the gains, investing in the household economy to protect them from bearing the costs of the transformation as much as possible and, above all, ensuring that the new growth that is unleashed not only does not add to environmental risk, but actively begins to reduce it.

As in past transformations many jobs, communities and households are going to be affected by the changes. Populist nationalists like Bannon and Trump want traditional jobs to be protected. A country isn't a country if it no longer produces steel, as Trump has tweeted. But such gestures will ultimately prove futile and, to the extent that they are successful, slow down the recovery. Some of the new technologies may be a much better way of saving and even rebuilding a manufacturing sector than using protectionist policies. From a household and biosphere perspective a new wave of growth based on these new technologies may be preferable to the alternative, but only if the new wealth and capabilities that are created are used to tackle environmental dangers and improve the wellbeing of households. These are, though, not the metrics by which economic policy is usually assessed.

A NEW ECONOMIC MODEL

A new economic model is possible, to replace the one which crashed so spectacularly in 2008. There is an abundance of new thinking on the progressive left about what that model should include.

Progressives should embrace, not seek to block, the next wave of technological innovations. They also need a compelling story to explain how they plan to avoid some of the big problems associated with the finance-led growth model of the 1990s. These plans include ensuring that any further economic growth is sustainable and aimed at reducing environmental risk rather than increasing it; adopting policies which can reverse the trend to greater inequality; marking much more clearly the boundaries of the market; decentralising the economy and empowering households; and changing the way corporations behave by reforming corporate governance.

The most important of these is the first – ensuring that any new growth model is environmentally sustainable in the sense that it does not continue to do increasing and possibly irreversible damage to the eco-systems that support life on this planet. More effective coordination of efforts to set limits to greenhouse gas emissions has begun, most notably in the Paris agreements in 2015. But many doubt that the steps being taken are large enough to be effective in the short time that may be left, and in any case the US, one of the two biggest sources of greenhouse gas emissions, has been pulled out of the accords by Trump.

Table 3.1 shows the environmental boundaries within which humanity can operate safely.

Action to achieve such a complex goal as energy security will require concerted international action, but it also needs a domestic strategy. Green growth will need to be embedded in national economic plans, and will have to develop through many experiments and initiatives, particularly at the local level. The whole society needs to be enlisted in finding solutions to the environmental challenge, because democratic consent will be vital. It can already be seen in small ways like the campaign to reduce the use of plastics, which contaminate rivers and oceans. While governments need to be active in creating legal and fiscal frameworks to encourage changes in behaviour by domestic households and businesses of all kinds, they also need to intervene much more directly to determine outcomes. The sociologist Tony Giddens has pointed to the paradox

Table 3.1. Environmental boundaries within which humanity can operate safely

Earth system processes	Parameter	Boundary	Current level
Climate change	Atmospheric CO_2 (parts per million)	350	>400
Biodiversity loss	Extinction rate (no. of species per million per year)	10	>100
Nitrogen cycle	Amount of nitrogen removed from the atmosphere for human use (million tonnes per year)	35	>120
Freshwater use	Human consumption of freshwater (km^3 per year)	4000	c.3000
Ocean acidification	Global mean saturation state of aragonite in surface sea water	2.75	2.9
Landmass usage	Global landmass used for crops (%)	15	c.12

Source: Hay, C and Payne, A (2015) Civic Capitalism.

that because the dangers posed by global warming are not immediate or visible to most people they ignore them in their daily lives. At the same time, waiting for them to become visible and immediate before taking serious action will by definition be too late. This is one area where a much more interventionist state seems inevitable. But there is another paradox. Such a state will only be accepted by citizens if they become convinced of the need to change their own behaviour and want help from the state in doing so. This is an area like seat belts or bans on smoking in public places where the state has to take a lead, for example by investing in renewable sources of energy and speeding up the introduction of electric cars.

A new economic model also needs a strategy for marking the boundaries of the market. Competitive markets in a globalised trading sector are a key part of a successful economy, but if not carefully regulated they tend to invade spheres from which they should be excluded. The idea that everything is potentially for sale has to be rejected. Three decades of the economic liberalism which became the new orthodoxy in the 1980s has pushed the boundaries too far. Outsourcing and privatisation have invaded the local economy, creating a number of predator private monopolies, like Carillion in the UK, which serve their shareholders rather than local communities, and load extra costs on to households and the local economy. The idea of the commons – protected public spaces applied, for example, to knowledge and scientific research, and to the genome and public service media – are also of vital importance. There are many areas of life where competitive markets have no place and are harmful. Apart from some Chicago economists few would think it a good idea to make personal relationships in the family subject to the price mechanism and market exchange. Where the boundaries are to be drawn precisely at any one time is a political question and there is an important principle too. There are certain spaces, including the family, households, many key goods and services in the local economy, and the public domain, where market forces should not hold sway. This rebalancing of the economy in favour of households and the everyday economy, the economics of place, communities and localities is one of the big changes an Open Left agenda should support.

A third area for a progressive political economy is its strategy for innovation. Everyone wants a knowledge-based economy, but a knowledge-based economy for what? A progressive political economy should steer investment guided by overriding purposes of safeguarding the biosphere for future generations, and promoting the wellbeing of all households, particularly those with the least resources and opportunities. All progressive critiques of our current political economy agree that there needs to be a rebalancing between the kind of short-term financial investment promoted by some parts of the City of London, and the long-term committed investment which successful industrial companies need, and which the journalist and political economist Will Hutton, among others, has written about so eloquently. One recent example is the attempted takeover of GKN, one of the UK's oldest engineering companies, by Melrose, a City investment company which specialises in buying companies, reorganising them, and selling them on. GKN, which has been resisting the takeover, is a major supplier to Airbus. Airbus has warned publicly that if the Melrose deal goes through, it may have to look elsewhere for the parts it needs, because it believes Melrose is only interested in short-term profits and would starve GKN of the long-term investment it needs to remain a leading supplier of aerospace parts. Many of the shareholders which sold their shares to Melrose had only bought into GKN in the weeks preceding the hostile takeover because they knew they could make a quick profit. This has happened over and over again in Britain's industrial history. There is increasing agreement on all sides of politics that change is needed. A way must be found of protecting what remains of the UK's industrial base from hostile takeovers, giving it the support and long-term commitment it needs to stay competitive. This is a role for the kind of entrepreneurial state and new form of industrial strategy envisaged by the economists Michael Jacobs and Mariana Mazzucato.

Another important avenue to explore is the potential to build a much more decentralised economy, particularly in parts of the local economy, but also in some globalised sectors. An Open Left should champion entrepreneurship and small companies, and the building of a network of regional banks to support them. The economy needs a much more diverse ecology of businesses, including not-for-profit companies, mutuals and cooperatives, but also many of the new sharing enterprises which are developing. This is a vital, growing part of the economy and it promises to unlock a stream of important innovations as the digital economy develops. Matthew Taylor, the chief executive of the Royal Society of Arts (RSA), and the journalists Charlie Leadbeater and Paul Mason among others have highlighted the progressive potential of the sharing economy to enable greater economic and social participation.

Support should also be given to experiments like that in Preston, where a local community has begun attempting to localise wealth, trying to prevent money leaking out of the community. In 2013 only £1 for every £20 spent stayed in Preston. By persuading public bodies in the city to spend more of their budgets locally a big boost has been given to the creation of new small businesses and worker cooperatives providing goods and services for the local economy. Such companies put money back into the local economy rather than taking it out. The results so far have been impressive. Instead of money being sucked out of local economies by large national and international firms, with their headquarters and shareholders located elsewhere, more of the money generated locally is retained locally, boosting employment and prosperity. Finance is raised for local development without having to rely on the City of London. In this way local economies can regain some independence and confidence. Smaller cities like Preston have often been the most disadvantaged in the globalisation era. Investment goes to the big cities at the centre of regional hubs and to global cities like London. The citizens who are most disaffected from politics, and most resentful of social change including immigration, tend to live in the smaller towns and cities. Finding a way to rebuild these local economies by providing more jobs and creating more local businesses can help restore a sense of local pride. This is a crucial step in forming a wider consensus for progressive change.

A fifth area for progressive political economy is corporate governance. The power of corporations in the modern economy has grown to the point where many markets are dominated by a few big players. Governments rely on big corporations for the smooth operation of the economy, but these corporations also rely on the government to make their operations possible. It is often forgotten that the scale of corporations we have today was only made possible by the grant of limited liability in the 1850s. Before that the directors of companies had an absolute liability if the company failed. They could not just walk away. The granting of limited liability was eventually conceded against some fierce opposition in order to make possible the raising of capital for the kind of large-scale undertakings like railway construction which the industrial economies increasingly required. In the UK limited liability was a legal form. It conferred a licence to operate while still treating the company as a private association. In Germany the law conceived the company as a public association with obligations and duties to the public as well as rights. For a progressive political economy the company is too important an institution to be treated as though it were a private association with no obligations to the rest of the community. That has begun to change but needs to go much further and be embodied in new legislation on corporate governance, which British governments have always avoided.

The priority given to maximising shareholder value to the exclusion of all other stakeholders in the company needs to change. Companies are key strategic actors in markets, but they cannot be allowed to operate just as private associations. They must recognise their wider obligations as well. We need to revive the ideas of stakeholding, putting workers and other stakeholders on the boards of public companies and ensuring that companies have a statutory duty to maximise wider stakeholder value. Shareholders are also stakeholders, but their interests should not be the only ones considered when deciding takeovers, remuneration and corporate strategy. If firms were obliged to maximise stakeholder value they would have to take into account the impact of their activities on the household economy, the local economy and the green economy. This would be an important step in correcting some of the imbalances which have emerged.

Finally, there is rising inequality, another negative outcome of the economic liberalism of the last three decades. Postwar there was a substantial reduction in income and wealth inequality but this trend was reversed from the 1980s onwards, as a byproduct of the new policy regime established in the US and the UK, which permeated all western democracies. There were large increases in inequality in many countries, including Germany and Sweden. But it was in the Anglo-Saxon countries where the excesses were most marked. Using their structural market power, banks, transnational companies and many other large bureaucratic organisations, including many in the public sector, exploited their position and, using the excuse of international market forces, increased pay and bonuses of executives to dizzying heights. In many banks and corporations the ratio in the income paid to the chief executive officer and the lowest paid worker reached 400:1. These were rents, extracted from businesses by a corporate culture dedicated to self-enrichment. Few things have done more to fuel populist anger than the bonuses which bankers felt entitled to award themselves both before the crash and after it. The remedies lie in reforming corporate governance and changing the way individuals and corporates are taxed. Much more needs to be done, in conjunction with other states, to close down offshore tax havens, to oblige all companies operating in the UK to pay tax, and to close loopholes. It has often been said that there is one welfare state for ordinary citizens and another for corporate citizens. These are two very different kinds of household and they are treated very differently by the state. There is also scope for new property taxes, like a land value tax, and for the reform of existing property taxes, like council tax, based on new bands reflecting current rather than historical valuations. These would have the advantage of providing an independent fiscal base for local government. The operation of other taxes, including inheritance tax and capital gains tax, should be reviewed.

Figure 3.3 shows the Gini index after housing costs in the UK between 1961 and 2011. The Gini coefficient represents income inequality across the population as a figure between 0 (where every individual has the same income) and 1 (where one individual has all the income).

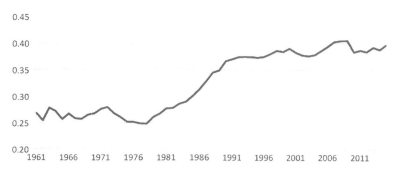

Figure 3.3 Gini index after housing costs in the UK, 1961–2015. *Source*: Institute for Fiscal Studies, Living Standards, Poverty and Inequality in the UK, 1961–2015.

The problem of inequality is a wider challenge in our contemporary political economy. It illustrates the unchecked nature of corporate and financial power. Many of the previous constraints and countervailing forces which existed have been swept away by the reforms of the last three decades. Inequality helped deliver an economy which grew steadily and provided a growth dividend to fund the expansion of public services. But this all came crashing down in 2008. In an era of austerity there is even less justification for discrepancies in wealth and income. A return to a more egalitarian ethos is overdue, and essential if trust in the way the economy is run and managed is to be restored.

WELFARE

Since the 2008 financial crash welfare states have been under pressure. But this is not new. Welfare states have been under pressure since the period of stagflation in the 1970s when it was questioned whether western economies could any longer afford their welfare states. They have grown considerably since then and now the question is being raised again, in this new period of austerity and recession. No one doubts that we need welfare, in the broad meaning of the term: the state or condition of doing or being well. No one in politics seriously wants the opposite. But do we need a welfare state to provide it? Cannot welfare be organised in other ways, through markets and individual choice, like any other goods which people want? This is the intellectual challenge which economic liberals and libertarians have been mounting.

There are also political and policy clouds over the welfare state, particularly in a time of austerity. Are some of its programmes, particularly the open-ended universal programmes like healthcare, still affordable? Are taxpayers collectively prepared to pay enough to support the quality and range of services they expect? There is a paradox of modern welfare states. The richer societies become the less able or willing they seem to be to fund welfare collectively.

Another concern about the contemporary welfare state is whether it is capable of being reformed to adjust to the new era of the digital economy and rapidly changing work patterns and lifestyles. Some writers on the welfare state think it is a doomed enterprise, despite the enormous effort which has gone into rethinking, redesigning and reorganising the welfare state in the last 30 years. The political scientist Paul Pierson has pictured the welfare state as a Maginot Line, all its guns pointing the wrong way. It has become too cumbersome, too bureaucratic, too sclerotic to be reformed. It is fated to become obsolete in a fast-changing society.

Despite all this gloom the welfare state remains one of the big achievements of the 20th century. The limited welfare states sponsored for national security reasons by conservative politicians like Otto von Bismarck and Liberal politicians like Joseph Chamberlain were eclipsed by the new vision of democratic citizenship championed by progressive parties, looking to add social rights to the political and civil rights already won. By the middle of the 20th century to have established an extensive welfare state was recognised as an indicator of success and maturity, the way in which the class tensions of earlier decades could be overcome and a lasting settlement between capital and labour achieved. The property rights of capital were protected in exchange for the state ensuring that all citizens would have access to universal public services providing the best possible healthcare, education, housing and income support.

This expansion of the welfare state after 1945 in all the western democracies was a signal progressive achievement, and the welfare state became a key pillar of social democratic programmes. The way in which that was achieved further solidified the idea of progress with the extension of government. In Britain the change was particularly remarkable. State spending grew as a percentage of national income from below 10% before 1914 to an average of 25% in the 1920s and 1930s and then to an average of 40% after 1945 (Figure 4.1). The public household became much more complex and required much higher levels of taxation to finance all its activities. The scope and scale of government was very different from the

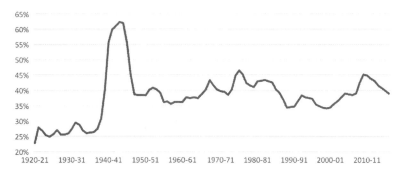

Figure 4.1 Total managed expenditure in the UK (% of GDP), 1920/21–2016/17. *Source*: Office for Budget Responsibility, Public Finances Databank, 1920/21–2016/17.

previous century and the expansion of the welfare state was one of its most important components. Governments also now took responsibility for managing the economy in a much more active way, and for investing in infrastructure, science, innovation and skills.

This high point proved temporary because, with the slowing of the western economy in the 1970s and with governments struggling with to keep inflation under control, the welfare state became a target of attack from both left and right. The left argued that capitalism could no longer afford the welfare state, and that, in any case, the welfare states as they had developed were deeply flawed because they had become agencies of social control, stigmatising and disciplining claimants and loading costs on to households and women. The right agreed that capitalism could no longer afford the welfare state, arguing that welfare states have become engines for destroying prosperity rather than sustaining it. Welfare spending had become a burden and resources were misallocated because there was no proper market discipline or budget constraint. In the UK the problem was often blamed on the retreat from the original insurance principle proposed by William Beveridge for the welfare state, which related benefits to contributions. In other European welfare states, where the insurance principle had been better preserved, this criticism had less force. In the UK many on the right argued that because welfare had come to be funded increasingly from general taxation it was viewed by many citizens as an entitlement regardless of contribution. There was also the argument, particularly popular in the US, that welfare spending infantilised the poor, breeding dependence and cycles of deprivation.

Radical right rather than radical left governments were elected in the 1980s, particularly in the English-speaking countries, and there was a concerted move towards a much more residual welfare state, trying to focus provision primarily on income support, and then only on the poorest. Much more generous provision persisted in the Nordic countries and in Germany, France and the Benelux countries. Even in the residual welfare states there were still programmes to combat insecurity arising in the life cycle and the labour market, and important universal programmes like the NHS. The radical right governments encountered strong resistance to welfare retrenchment and their success in rolling back the state, as they had boasted, was quite limited, especially in relation to the big universal programmes. There was more success in reducing programmes which only benefited minorities. However, a lot of reshaping and redesign of public services took place, with the rise of the new public management and its targets, quasi-markets and audit culture. New measures of efficiency were introduced in a bid to cut costs and keep the lid on rising expenditure, but these efforts were only partially successful.

A third phase in the development of the welfare state began in the mid-1990s. In reaction to the policies which had promoted residualisation and attempted rollback of the welfare state, a new programme of social investment emerged. This argued for a smart enabling state, which could rethink the welfare state, adapting it to new circumstances including globalisation, the loss of so many manufacturing jobs in the move to service economies, and the new social risks associated with changed lifestyles and patterns of living. The social investment strategy for the welfare state put the emphasis on helping individuals navigate the frequent changes in the labour market and the course of their own lives, investing in every individual in order to raise the quality of the stock of human capital and the capabilities of every citizen. At the same time, a commitment to social investment went hand in hand with maintaining strong minimum income universal safety nets, which offered social protection and acted as economic stabilisers. This period had its critics at the time, many arguing that it adopted many of the methods and tools which had been developed by the free-market right in the 1980s and 1990s, and helped to shore up the regime rather than challenge it. It was, though, hard to argue with some of the outcomes. In the UK spending on health and education between 2001 and 2008 rose at a faster rate than at any time since 1945 (Figure 4.2). As a share of GDP spending on the NHS rose from 5% to 8%. Many new and innovative social policies were trialled in this period, and minimum wage legislation was implemented.

The contrast with the period since 2008 is very marked. The economy in 2017 was 14% smaller than it would have been if growth had continued on its trajectory before the financial crash, and although some of the universal programmes like health and education were given some protection they still fell back as a proportion of

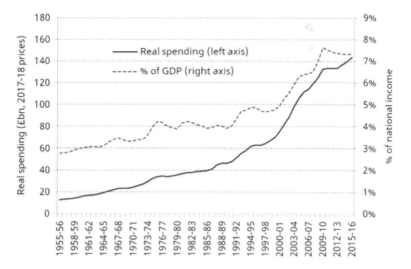

Figure 4.2 Public spending on health in the UK (% of national income), 1955/56–2015/16. *Source*: © Institute for Fiscal Studies, IFS Briefing *Note* BN201.

national income. Many other programmes, particularly those funded and administered by local authorities, were cut back drastically. Many disappeared altogether. Voluntary organisations which relied on local authority grants lost this financial support and many have struggled to survive. The policies which have been pursued to bring down the deficit such as austerity and quantitative easing have distributed most of the costs of dealing with the financial crisis on to households, and therefore on to women as the main carers for both the young and the old. Austerity in the form of spending cuts and pay freezes has hit the living standards of the majority hard, while those with assets have benefited from quantitative easing; the value of those assets has been maintained and substantially increased in real terms over the period. The end of the growth dividend for the public finances also ended the debates on whether it should be used to cut taxes or boost spending. It was replaced by debates on austerity: who should bear the biggest burden, and how should the pain be spread between raising taxes and cutting spending.

There were always different ways to tackle austerity, although governments often pretended otherwise. All countries were forced to make adjustments because of the sharp drop in output, but countries chose very different mixes of spending cuts, tax increases and borrowing. Sweden chose to have no fiscal squeeze at all, while the UK and Lithuania among EU states chose in their fiscal squeezes to have very high ratios, over 90%, of spending cuts to tax increases. The political issue then and now, since austerity is still not over given the very high debt levels, is not austerity as such but what kind of austerity. Welfare spending was targeted in many austerity programmes but not all welfare spending. The selectivity of cuts reflected political priorities.

The sustained attack on many welfare programmes was accompanied by the revival of aggressive discourses targeting welfare claimants, and by arguments that the welfare state had outlived its usefulness. Suitable for an era of industrial capitalism, collective organisation and patriarchal households in the 20th century, it no longer made sense for the new forms of entrepreneurial and digital capitalism which were emerging. With the politics of austerity came the rise of new anti-welfare coalitions. The attraction of low taxes or even flat taxes, removing all progressive elements in taxation, gained popularity. Welfare could be contracted for like any other service. A key argument of those in the US opposed to Obamacare has been why should you be made to insure yourself if you are healthy? Every individual should decide what their own level of risk is and take out health insurance accordingly. The attack on welfare in the years of austerity has been particularly focused on non-universal benefits, such as social security, and reflects an undermining of that sense of collective solidarity and common purpose, which was such an important underpinning of the welfare state in the past (Figure 4.3).

It is easy to exaggerate the strength of the anti-welfare coalition. Most populist nationalists are staunch defenders of welfare programmes, at least for those they define as their people, part of their nation. Electorates are still very reluctant to vote for the dismantling of the big universal programmes of the welfare state,

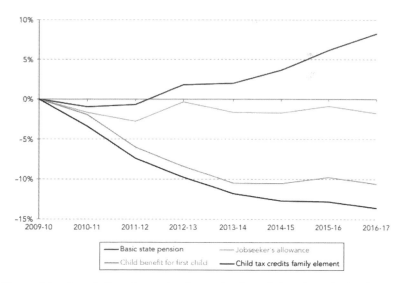

Figure 4.3 Cumulative change in the real value of four benefits in the UK, 2009/10–2016/17 (CPI adjusted). *Source*: Corlett, A and Clarke, S (2017) Living Standards, Resolution Foundation.

although many programmes for minorities have been drastically pruned. All the same, there is no denying how fragile the welfare state has become. How should an Open Left respond?

There are several key issues it must confront. The first is afford-ability. The growth of tax resistance among voters and increasing levels of tax avoidance and evasion by companies and individu-als have contributed to a shrinking of the tax base which has put government spending programmes under pressure, particularly in a period of austerity. The gulf has grown between what voters will pay in taxes and the quality and range of the services they expect. This gap has always been there but in a more individualist and con-sumerist culture the desire to have your cake and eat it has grown. If it gets too wide this is an impossible divide for governments to straddle, particularly for progressive parties. Either taxes must be raised or spending cut, or the government must incur additional bor-rowing. The dilemma is acute. When growth was stronger before 2008 progressive governments could fudge the issue by a mixture of stealth taxes, extra borrowing and the use of the extra resources each year from the growth of the economy. The stagnation of pro-ductivity and the slow rate of growth of output since then has made the choices much tougher. Centre-right governments across Europe used a discourse about the need to reduce the deficit to paint their political opponents as deficit deniers, even though the economic case for austerity was always weak and, as the IMF has recently argued, needlessly reduced the rate of growth and the pace of the recovery. But once the issue was successfully framed as the deficit, and it was accepted that the only responsible way to bear down on the deficit was to cut spending rather than increase taxes, it became very hard for any opposing party advocating something different to appear economically credible. Only now, a decade after the crash, is the grip of austerity weakening, and the case for trying to stimulate a much faster rate of growth through government action has become more acceptable on both left and right.

Yet even if we assumed that the optimists are right and that we are on the edge of a new period of sustained growth, the dilemma does not go away. Populist nationalists like Trump are quite happy to push a Reaganite supply-side agenda of big tax cuts, particularly for the rich, and big spending increases as a way to stimulate the economy. This can certainly provide a short-term boost, but it is based on the false expectation that tax cuts and spending increases will pay for themselves out of the proceeds of economic growth. In the 1980s they led directly to large deficits and the trillion dollar debt which helped lose George Bush re-election in 1992. It also widened inequality. A progressive programme for sustainable growth has to have a plan to balance the economy.

The problem of the affordability of public services needs to be met in two ways. Health services should give greater emphasis to preventative medicine and become more decentralised, particularly in countries like the UK. Fiscal and regulatory measures can help shift the behaviour of food manufacturers and citizens on issues like excess sugar in food and drink, which is responsible for so many health problems. Decentralisation of health services would also help relieve pressure on hospitals. The experience of introducing private providers has had mixed results but that is no reason to recentralise. There should instead by more experiments with a range of providers, particular cooperatives and non-profitmaking organisations.

The second way of dealing with affordability is to increase taxes, and not just on the rich, but on the majority. The situation is already serious but it will get worse because of the rising tide of expectations and entitlements, together with the tendency for costs to increase faster in the public sector than outside it. The biggest problems lie in the commitments to open-ended universal benefits, the cost of health treatments, as a result of medical advances, and the cost of pensions, as people live longer. The actuarial assumptions on which many schemes were founded have proved unrealistic. If the basic principles of a welfare state providing services for all and free at the point of use are to be sustained, then electorates have to be per-suaded to pay more, as they have been doing for a long time in the Nordic countries, either indirectly through consumption taxes such as a sugar tax, or directly through income tax or national insurance contributions. The alternative is that the quality of services provided collectively deteriorates, and individuals start paying privately for better quality. To avoid this slippery slope the fiscal foundations of some of the main welfare services have to be made more robust. It is a challenge which very few centre-left parties want to take on. In the UK the Liberal Democrats have been the boldest with their proposals for a hypothecated tax to pay for the NHS. There is now an acceptance across all parties of the need to raise more funding to pay for the NHS. This is a moment progressives should seize.

A second issue which an Open Left must confront is competitiveness. During the era of globalisation the goal of full employment was abandoned and organised labour weakened. At times it has sparked anxieties about a race to the bottom, particularly in labour and welfare standards. If companies can locate their production anywhere in the world, and outsource their activities to where costs of labour and raw materials are lowest, then how can citizens of any country defend high wages and a generous welfare state? The experience of globalisation has shown that there is no simple relationship between more open economies and a race to the bottom. Some of the most successful economies in the globalisation era have been relatively small economies, which have maintained both high wages and a generous welfare state. They have managed to do this not by protectionist measures to stop outsoucing and the entry of cheaper products into their markets, but by investing in the skills of their workers, households and the reproductive economy, and moving to higher value manufacturing and specialised services, a classic social investment strategy.

Competitiveness remains a serious challenge for a progressive political economy because of other impacts of globalisation. It reinforces the transnational nature of capital while underlining the national character of welfare states. The conflict this sets up was explored in chapter 2. The encouragement of flexible labour markets and freedom of movement boosts immigration. There is a push and pull factor. Employers seek to recruit large numbers of immigrant workers to fill skill shortages partly because of their skills and personal qualities (they are willing to work hard and for long hours) and partly because of the wages they will work for compared with domestic workers. Economic migrants themselves are attracted by the employment opportunities and the level of wages in rich countries. The level of welfare benefits is not a significant factor, since generally the purpose of being an economic migrant is to earn as high a wage as possible in order to send remittances home; access to housing and healthcare are more important. However, as already noted, the presence of large numbers of migrants is a source of tension with local communities, and has fueled resentments that have fed the identity politics on which populist nationalists have thrived. Many economies with flexible labour markets, including that of the UK, have become very dependent on immigrant labour to keep their economies expanding and dynamic. It was an important part of the growth model, and turning it off would either damage growth, and with it the fiscal basis for the welfare state, or would require employers to invest heavily in training domestic workers for the skills they need. A progressive political economy should go as far as possible down the second route, ending the reliance on an economy of low-paid and low-skill employment. Local communities need reassurance that the flow of migrants is under the control of their government, rather than being something it either cannot or will not control. Any attempt to go further and institute closed borders would be counter-productive though. The economy must remain open, and a high level of immigration is desirable and beneficial to an advanced economy. An Open Left has to be prepared to engage in difficult conversations over the level of taxation and the level of immigration.

As discussed in the last chapter, one of the reasons why it is difficult to discuss immigration is that the levels of wages and social wages (public services and welfare benefits) in the rich democracies are a form of economic rent and economic privilege, which has resulted from two centuries of unequal economic development. One of the forces holding them up is the nation state. But it is not certain that can always be done. There is no prior right which ensures that the way the world's resources and wealth have been distributed in the modern era will continue. There is a difficult balance to strike, between protecting the incomes and prospects of existing populations, while doing everything possible to help the rest of the world to improve their incomes and prospects at the same time. A race to the bottom helps no one, but neither do closed policies adopted by the rich countries to protect themselves.

Affordability and competitiveness are the two toughest dilemmas a progressive strategy for the welfare state must confront. In neither case will winning electoral support for a policy of raising taxes to fund the welfare state, whether through hypothecated taxes or general taxation, or for a controlled but liberal immigration policy, be easy. They are only likely to succeed if put within the framework of a broad vision for renewing the economy, rebuilding the welfare state, extending democracy, and committing to multilateral institutions to resolve conflicts. Strategy towards the welfare state cannot simply be defensive. It has to offer a vision of how the welfare state can evolve and change to meet new circumstances. Many of the risks that citizens and households face are old ones – job insecurity, illness, insufficient skills and opportunities, lack of resources. But there are new risks as well, arising from the changing patterns of work and households, including the number of single parents and workless households, and the precarious nature of so many jobs. Without effective trade unions in many parts of the economy workers often face zero-hour contracts, temporary work and few employment rights. Women's participation rate has risen steadily, but the burden of social care of the elderly falls disproportionately on women, who tend to be concentrated in low-paid and often part-time employment. Figure 4.4 shows how trade union membership in Great Britain has declined since 1989.

Some of the other big changes that have been taking place include the shift from manufacturing to services. This is occurring in all the advanced economies, but at a faster pace in some than others. In the UK already 80% of the workforce are employed in services rather than manufacturing. This is as big and important a shift as the earlier

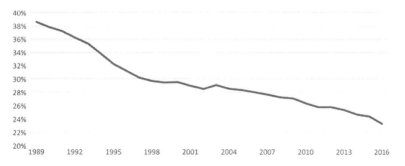

Figure 4.4   Trade union membership as a percentage of employees, Great Britain, 1989–2016. *Source*: ONS, Trade Union Membership 2016: Statistical Bulletin.

shift from agriculture to manufacturing. One of the most prominent aspects of the service economy is financialisation. Citizens are increasingly treated, and see themselves, as autonomous financial agents who must incur substantial debts at different stages of their lives. This trend is associated with the rise of a more individualist society and political culture, and a corresponding weakening of the institutions that used to nurture social solidarity, such as trade unions, churches, extended families, large factories and working-class communities. Evidence from British Social Attitudes surveys shows that during the austerity years there was a marked hardening of attitudes towards the poor and declining support for redistribution.

Another major trend has been changes in the demographic profile of the western nations. People are living longer and infant mortality has been brought down to very low levels. These trends reflect improving medical knowledge and interventions, as well as better nutrition, housing, air quality, health and safety legislation, and a much greater awareness of risks to health from lifestyle choices such as smoking, and environmental risks such as air pollution. These trends have not come about by accident. They are the result of decades of fighting for and successfully implementing progressive policies, often in the face of strong opposition from particular producer interests and conservative lobby groups. There are many more battles to fight and many of those already won are not guaranteed to stay won. A determined government, like the Trump administration in the US, can roll them back.

One of the biggest issues these changes raise is a growing split between the generations. Several factors have contributed to redistribution increasingly take place from young to old. This has been exacerbated by political parties becoming very sensitive to the concerns of the older generations, mindful of how much more likely older people are to vote than younger people. Older people by living longer are also making up more of the population. Not only is there a problem that the old tend to be asset rich and the young asset poor and that the gap between them is increasing. There is also the issue that the number of citizens who are working and paying taxes may start decreasing as a proportion of the population, particularly if immigration is cut back sharply. There is a case for looking again at some of the special tax privileges and benefits older people receive, and at the same time tackling more vigorously the main problems young people face. In some countries like the UK affordable housing is perhaps the main concern; in others, like Spain or Italy, unemployment among young people is the crucial issue. What is undeniable is that western societies are inexorably ageing, which can have negative effects for the economy, politics and culture. There are solutions, but none of them are of the kind politicians normally want to think about. Raising the retirement age is one, which all countries have embarked on, but very gradually. Then there is immigration. The quickest way to raise the proportion of younger people in the population is to open the borders. That is hardly a vote-winner just now. There are also policies to raise the birth rate, but these again are slow-acting and in the past have not proved very effective.

Another big issue for an Open Left is social mobility. In many countries, including the UK, social mobility has declined. The reasons are complex, and have been explored in depth by the Social Mobility Commission in its regular reports. They find that in the UK there is a stark social mobility postcode lottery. The chances of someone from a disadvantaged background succeeding depends on where they live. The most striking geographical divide is between

London and the rest of the country. Many places in Britain, particularly rural and coastal areas and the towns of Britain's old industrial heartlands, are being left behind economically and hollowed out. These disturbing findings show the importance of reviving the local economies of these areas, as Preston is managing to do. Much higher government investment is needed but also local initiatives aimed at improving job prospects, child support and education for the most deprived areas. Equal opportunities have long been a central goal of progressive politics. There has been great success in opening up higher education to almost 50% of school-leavers, but access to higher education for those from disadvantaged backgrounds remains a problem. Much more needs to be done to create career paths and train the half of 18-year-olds who do not go on to university. The evidence on social mobility which the commission has presented in its reports helps explain part of the background to the Brexit vote. A priority for any progressive government has to be to close the gaps that are opening up between different parts of the country, and even within some of the richest areas.

THE FUTURE OF THE WELFARE STATE

The future of the welfare state is stronger than it sometimes appears because, although battered, the broad coalition in most western democracies in support of welfare services that are universal and free at the point of use is still intact. No democracy which has established a mature welfare state has so far abandoned it. This is partly because voters will not support a party that tries to dismantle key public services on which a majority of people have come to rely. This is true even in the US with programmes like Medicare, and it is why it is proving so difficult for Trump to get rid of Barack Obama's Affordable Care Act.

But there are other reasons too. There is a mutual dependence between capitalist market economies and the welfare state. It is often said by economic liberals that the welfare state needs capitalism, in the sense that the welfare state depends on the wealth which capitalism creates. But it is equally true that capitalism needs the welfare state, which is why so many of the early initiatives to create welfare states came from the right as much as from the left. The welfare state helped to promote social stability and the legitimacy of government. As argued in the previous chapter, capitalist markets have always needed institutions outside markets themselves, and organised on very different principles, in order to survive and expand. These non-market institutions are the households, public, corporate and domestic, which are both strategic actors within markets and the absorbers of losses and the distributors of burdens. The complex institutional networks of advanced welfare states provide key public goods such as education, health, skills, childcare and adult social care, which underpin the flexible labour markets of modern societies. Markets will not provide these as effectively and certainly not as comprehensively. The cohesion of national communities in many countries has come to be defined by the collective commitment to provide all citizens with certain rights and opportunities. Does any politician want to go back to the undernourished, undereducated, unhealthy, insecure proletariats of the 19th century? Some of the hidden costs after 100 years of industrial progress under the aegis of economic liberalism were exposed in Britain at the start of the first world war after conscription was announced. Large numbers of working-class recruits were found to be medically unfit for military service.

The welfare state faces an intellectual, political and policy challenge but also a deeper moral one. The social contract between the state and its citizens which underpins the modern welfare state needs renewing in every generation. The kind of welfare state a society has defines what it means to be a citizen in that democracy. If the welfare state is not strong, democracy and the legitimacy of capitalist market institutions are put at risk. The key foundation of a strong welfare state are policies and institutions which give precedence to the citizenship rights of individuals over their market performance. For example, everyone has a right to healthcare and education regardless of their income or the income of their family. For such rights to be recognised there has to be a sense of community and solidarity. If that gets eroded the welfare state can start to shrink, reducing its coverage of individuals, and encouraging individuals to do much more for themselves rather than collectively. The boundary is not fixed and can shift over time, but what is important for the idea of a welfare state is the widespread acceptance that there is such a boundary and that it should be preserved.

The basic principles underlying the welfare state must be upheld, but an Open Left will always be alive to new possibilities and new ways of improving the coverage of the welfare state and the quality of the services it delivers. There is still great potential in the social investment strategy of the 1990s and early 2000s in seeking to combine protection and opportunity. But it is also important to learn from some of its mistakes. It tended to focus on new social risks rather than older social risks. That may have been right at the time, but since the crash that emphasis has needed correcting, as there is increasing poverty and unemployment in many democracies. In some of the policies pursued higher-income groups benefited much more than lower-income groups. This has long been a feature of welfare states, which requires attention. Many of the social investments made in the good times were overshadowed, and in some cases nullified, by the effects of austerity.

It is clear from the experience of austerity in the last 10 years that full employment should be reconsidered. It was abandoned as a target in the 1980s, and as the economy was restructured unemployment climbed to very high levels. In the 1990s, with the globalisation boom in the international economy, unemployment fell in many countries, particularly those with flexible labour markets, and attention shifted to investment in the skills and capacities of all individuals to help them make the most of employment opportunities at different stages of their lives. But the experience of austerity, and the changes to come with the digital economy and artificial intelligence, require a rethink. The state needs to become more assertive in helping trade unions to become stronger and families more robust.

Above all what is needed are new visions of what democratic citizenship means in the digitalised economy, which is emerging with such speed. Universal basic income (UBI) is one of those visions. The idea has been around a long time but has acquired a new salience since the renewed onslaught and stigmatising of benefit claimants during austerity and the prospects of a digital economy which removes a big swathe of existing jobs. UBI has numerous critics who point out some of the practical obstacles to making it work. Would there be democratic consent for an unconditional rather than conditional basic income? How would the special needs of particular claimants be handled if all means testing was abolished? Would there still need to be a safety net for those who did not make good choices with their basic income?

UBI is no panacea that can by itself magically remove all the complex problems in matching resources to needs in the existing welfare state. Its importance is that it makes us reflect on the original purpose of the welfare state, allowing all individual citizens to make their own life choices, freed from the burden of insecurity arising out of unemployment, illness, poverty and the lack of opportunity, and freed from stigma. Some of the critics of UBI suggest that a better aim for progressives would be universal basic services, ensuring that the core services on which all citizens rely at some stage of their lives are provided universally and free at the point of use. Another important idea in recent years has been to introduce capital grants, seeking to build a third pillar of the welfare state in addition to income support and direct services to redistribute resources so as to equip all young adults with a level of assets which all upper and many middle-income families take for granted, and to redress some of the imbalance in resources which has arisen between the generations.

One of the main purposes of a progressive welfare state is not to make people dependent on the state but to give them the personal autonomy and resources they need to live independently and make their own choices. For this to be possible it is vital to ensure that the welfare state does not just help individuals to adapt to circumstances and opportunities but actively shapes those circumstances and opportunities. This requires an active state, which not only provides the safety nets and support of the traditional welfare state, but also brings forward changes to the regulation of labour markets, financial markets, housing markets and corporate governance, which provide the bedrock security citizens need to be self-reliant, confident and enterprising themselves in contemporary society. The aim of the welfare state has always been to leave no one behind. It needs restating today.

DEMOCRACY

Democracy is not doing well. Low levels of trust in politics and democratic institutions is nothing new, but current levels of disaffection with the way democracies work is troubling. All forms of representative democracy are particularly under attack. In mature and stable democracies a majority of voters used to believe that their representatives would generally do the right thing and would represent them, not be corrupt, self-serving or remote. There was also an expectation that they would be competent. In recent years there has been a series of scandals which have involved almost every major institution in the UK, weakening trust in the probity and competence of those who run them. But beyond the scandals there has also been a sense of a widening gulf been voters and their representatives. The remoteness of political elites is often cited. Politicians are more remote in two senses. They have come to form a professional caste, with different experiences, interests and preoccupations from most of their fellow citizens. They are also grappling with highly complex policy issues, which most voters do not take the trouble to inform themselves about. Of course, politicians are still blamed when things go wrong.

How might trust be restored in representative democracy? For an Open Left it is an urgent question. If there is little popular respect for democratic institutions and democratic representatives it becomes much harder to achieve progressive aims, since these rely on belief in the possibility of change and change for the better. If voting does not change anything, if all politicians are corrupt, if there is nothing to choose between parties because they always implement the same policies, then most voters will be disengaged and apathetic, and resolve to pay even less attention to politics than they already do.

There has always been an argument that the more apathetic the electorate is the better, because it must suggest that voters are more or less happy with how they are being governed. The more politically engaged citizens are, the more must be at stake in elections. On this reasoning we should celebrate declining turnouts in elections as a sign of democratic health. But if governments are under no pressure to perform better they have little incentive to do so, and if voters are disengaged it leaves the field free for organised special interest groups to determine the shape and direction of government policy. The result is likely to be highly conservative and unadventurous. Reforms can be driven by a technocratic elite, but they will tend to be limited by conventional wisdom about what is politically possible. More ambitious reforms require popular involvement, protest and pressure, which helps redefine what is politically possible, and moves politics into a different place. Reforms can be reversed, or fail to deliver what they promised. Cycles of hope and disillusion seem intrinsic to politics. There is no guarantee of irreversible progress, but the progressive persuasion in politics has always believed that change is possible, and worth fighting for, even if the fight is never finished. For that to be realised, however, democracies have to be strong, not weak, and citizens have to have trust in their politicians.

An Open Left needs an open democracy, but the critique of what is wrong with our democracies goes much deeper than democratic deficits of trust and competence on the part of elites. Is there, after all, much good to say for the culture of modern democracies as they have turned out? Politicians and citizens alike seem to have little interest in evidence, and disregard it or misread it when it does not agree with other opinions or preconceptions they hold. This is happening even though we have more and better quality evidence than ever before from scientific research about which policies are likely to work and over what timescale, and which risks facing communities are greater and should be given priority. It seems remarkable, and is particularly frustrating for many scientists, that the evidence they provide can so lightly be set aside.

Psychologists have contributed a great deal to our understanding of the processes involved. The cognitive biases with which we interpret any new information and approach any new evidence make us all resistant to changing our minds when the facts change. We dispute that these are real facts, or reach for alternative facts. People have always tended to inhabit echo chambers in which their opinions are confirmed by what they read, what they see and who they interact with. Social media and the internet have taken echo chambers to a new level, though, by sealing people off if they so choose from contact with any opinions they do not share. The polarisation of opinion along identity lines is one of the most troubling features of modern democracies because it makes pragmatism and compromise in dealing with conflicts and divisions much harder. We should not exaggerate how new any of this. There have always been culture wars and fake news which have distorted democratic politics, but in recent times it has been amplified by the new media, because of its speed, immediacy and reach, which surpasses anything we had before.

Identity cultures are built on distinguishing friends from enemies, and on emphasising the things which a group has in common and distinguish it from those outside. They have always been one of the most important determinants of politics. National divides, cultural divides, ethnic divides, class divides, regional divides, religious divides and generational divides have all been important at different times and places. Political movements draw on these divides to build their support and define their purposes. Progressive movements are no different. It is wrong to imagine that there was ever a political culture based simply on interests, rationality, pragmatic calculation and compromise. Class politics had its own identity politics. What sometimes seems missing in contemporary politics is sufficient respect for the virtues of following the evidence and being ready to strike compromises to resolve conflicts. Politics has come to be dominated by concerns with identity rather than interest. Some proponents of identity politics are not dismayed if conflicts are never resolved, and that is what can make such politics so divisive and polarising. The search for common ground, even in the most divided communities, is an essential purpose for a progressive politics.

One of the weapons progressives have always relied on to dilute identity politics is freedom of speech, a culture of open, rational enquiry, the rule of law and a media which upholds all of these. One of the disturbing recent trends is the way so much of the media has itself become increasingly a tool of partisan identity politics. News stories are chosen and headlines slanted to appeal to a particular readership. The old distinction between news and opinion has long since disappeared. It can be argued that it was always a fiction, but it was also an ideal which many journalists strove to uphold. That has become increasingly hard today, and news is manipulated and framed more than ever before. Politics in the world of fake news becomes increasingly a politics of spectacle. It revolves around who can capture the attention of a disengaged and bored electorate. The complexity of modern government makes it hard to explain what government is doing and the constraints it faces. The answer of many charismatic politicians who want to connect directly with voters is to cut through the complexity, repeat simple truths and focus on what has emotional and shock appeal. Build that wall. Lock her up. Politicians learn that being knowledgeable, expert or competent in its traditional meaning can have disadvantages. It certainly makes a politician sound boring. Far better to be crass, outrageous and flamboyant.

Populist demagogues have always existed, so again the problem should not be exaggerated. It is as old as representative democracy itself. Democracy has always had its critics. Conservatives long opposed the extension of the vote to the working class and women, believing that it would end any prospect of good government, allowing policy to be dictated by the mob and manipulated by the demagogues who most successfully appealed to it. Today it is more often members of the liberal global elite, including many scientists and economists, who despair of the demos. Voters, they complain, are irrational, ill-informed, easily led and show poor judgement. Politicians reflect the biases and shortcomings of their voters, and as a result have no capacity or inclination to pursue long-term evidenced-based policies. Instead they are short term in their thinking and liable to promote schemes and policies which are not soundly based in evidence. Far better to take policymaking out of the hands of politicians and democratic electorates and instead entrust it to wise technocrats who can operate government in the public interest in the light of the best evidence of what works and what needs to be tackled.

Democracies are very imperfect forms of rule and frequently frustrating and obtuse. They are notoriously bad about thinking long term. As the political theorist David Runciman has argued, democracies tend to oscillate between drift and panic. There is an assumption that they will always end up doing the right thing, and take action to avert a catastrophe, but we cannot count on it. Yet the drawbacks of rule by technocrats unaccountable to the demos are even more unattractive. Such technocratic elites are unlikely to be progressive. They will by definition be authoritarian, and lacking checks and balances will be prone to corruption, manipulation and self-serving behaviour. The dream of an all-wise technocracy is a dream deep in the western political imagination. It reflects a desire for a world without politics and without conflict, in which everything could be ordered according to rational principles. But the world is not like that, and knowledge is not like that. We do not have certainty from any form of knowledge. The best we can hope for are systems which will allow rigorous checking of results, and opportunities to allow revision of results in the light of further evidence. Scientific inquiry is never complete and never reaches final conclusions, and is therefore best nurtured in an environment where the virtues of free speech, pluralism and diversity, and open enquiry are protected and actively celebrated. Human societies are characterised by deep divisions of interest, opinion and knowledge. The division of knowledge means that knowledge is decentralised, spread around many different groups because of their different circumstances and interests. None of this means we have to give up on the idea that some things are true and some are not. If we were to lose that distinction we really would be in trouble.

Acceptance that we cannot have certain knowledge, that there are no simple, objective answers, and that the truth is always going to be complicated are all essential starting points for an Open Left. It is one of the reasons democracy is so important. It is the culture of democracy, and the protection of civil and political freedoms, which are most vital in ensuring that processes of evidence-gathering and rational enquiry have some chance of survival. Democracy also implies that we should always be wary of too much centralisation of power. If knowledge is dispersed, power should be too. A strong democracy can give powers to the centre when that is appropriate but not as a first step. Decentralisation wherever possible is more likely to keep politicians accountable.

HOW SHOULD DEMOCRACY BE REFORMED?

If democracy is so important for any progressive political project how can it be strengthened? In every country there are specific issues and problems to be addressed, tied up with different national histories and institutions. Every country believes itself to be exceptional in some way. In the UK the peculiarities and idiosyncrasies of its constitutional development loom large. Some of the constitutional reforms advocated, like to the House of Lords, are still not complete after a century of failures and half measures. Reforming a constitution which rests on statute and precedent, has never been codified into a single document, and so can be interpreted in many different ways is always hard. The Labour government after 1997 brought in a raft of constitutional reforms from devolution of powers to Scotland

and Wales to freedom of information. Many of these reforms were intended to strengthen democracy and bring government closer to the people. Although reforms in the framework of government are important, measuring their effects is often difficult. They always make a big impact on the political class itself, but a much smaller one on citizens. The big exception in the Labour government's reforms were the devolution measures, which had strong support, especially in Scotland, were approved in referendums, and have irreversibly changed the constitution of the UK. In legal terms it is possible for a future UK government to repeal the Government of Scotland Act and the Government of Wales Act but it is not possible in political terms. Opinion in Wales and Scotland would be firmly against. The Scots and the Welsh may not be entirely content with their new institutions, turnout at elections remains relatively low, but large majorities would now resist any attempt to take them away.

One of the big constitutional issues which progressives have pushed in recent years is electoral reform. Few democracies use first past the post to decide their elections, preferring some form of proportional representation, but Britain, the US and a few other countries remain obstinately attached to it. One of the main differences which electoral systems have is how they affect the formation of governments. By more accurately reflecting how votes are cast, proportional systems produce parliaments in which a range of parties are represented, making coalition government the norm and single party government unusual. The parties have to negotiate with one another after an election to form a viable government. In first-past-the-post systems the winner takes all, and that usually ensures one party emerges from the election as a clear winner. The distribution of seats is not at all proportional to votes, which sometimes means the winning party secures a landslide of seats with well short of 50% of the vote. The party which wins the election usually has a clear majority in parliament and can therefore govern alone and get its programme through.

The main objection to the first-past-the-post system from an Open Left standpoint is that it artificially creates two large electoral coalitions which contest general elections. These coalitions are internally divided, so the negotiation between parties which happens in a proportional representation system happens in the UK within the parties rather than between them. In the 1950s and 1960s these two giant coalitions mopped up more than 90% of the vote. Since then, however, the vote for the two main parties has generally been well below 80% and in several elections below 70%. There was a recovery of the two main parties in 2017, but that election was heavily influenced by Brexit and the eclipse of smaller parties may not last.

A party system that does not properly represent the way citizens wish to cast their votes is poor and should be reformed. In societies that are increasingly divided on many different lines, a party system which reflects that diversity is more likely to encourage cooperation and consensus. The British system has always been highly adversarial. A proportional system makes it easier for parties to be pragmatic because they have to cooperate with one another in government. It is telling that proportional systems of different kinds have been adopted for the devolved parliaments and assemblies, as well as for elections to the European parliament. It is badly needed in local government in England (it was introduced in Scotland in 2002 and there are plans to do so in Wales). Under the first-past-the-post system one party often has almost a monopoly of the seats. It is a long overdue reform for the Westminster parliament.

Proportional representation would help make representative democracy more representative. It would not by itself solve the problem of the gap that has opened up between representatives and their electors. These problems are as acute in proportional representation systems as they are in first-past-the-post systems. The rise of professional politicians and cartel parties, controlled by their members or executives, make them increasingly insulated from their voters. Some observers think that there is no way that parties can again get in touch with their voters, and they propose radical solutions such as ending representative democracy altogether and introducing forms of direct democracy through referendums and, even better, online plebiscites. New media make possible direct citizen control, allowing the whole institutional structure of representative institutions and checks and balances to be swept aside. Some of the advocates of this new radical democracy argue that most of these institutions were designed, as in the US constitution, to prevent the direct expression of the popular will in government, rather than to enable it.

But no one has yet shown that direct democracy can be made to work in complex and diverse modern societies. Empowering temporary majorities through plebiscites risks disregarding minority interests and rights. Democracy is more than the popular will. It is also the political culture and the institutions which protect minorities and free speech, and promote peaceful change, negotiation and compromise. As the political scientist Albert Weale has recently pointed out, there is no such thing as the will of the people. It is a fiction used by populists. What was the will of the people in the Brexit referendum? Just under 52% voted leave and just over 48% remain; 28% of the electorate did not vote, so Brexit was carried with a vote of 37% of the whole electorate. Of that 37%, some who voted leave thought they were voting for a hard Brexit and Global Britain. Some thought they were voting for a soft Brexit with Britain staying in the customs union and the single market by joining European Free Trade Association. Some thought they were voting for a closing of the borders, sending all the foreigners home and getting British industries back and a big boost in spending to the NHS. Populist nationalists love plebiscites but they are a poor way of reaching decisions. Few policy issues can be expressed as binary choices, and attempting to do it in that way can lead to perverse outcomes. The experience of the Brexit referendum in the UK is not a particularly happy one. Such referendums can often divide and polarise communities in very damaging ways. If referendums are to be used they should be carefully defined in a country's constitution, specifying the type of issues and the procedures for holding them. They should not be made up in relation to the particular pressures within the ruling party.

Representation remains a valuable and indispensable principle for an Open Left. The voting system should be reformed, so that the distribution of seats in relation to votes is as fair as possible, and every effort made to keep a constituency link for most MPs. But we still do need those MPs. There has always been an argument about whether MPs should be delegates, taking detailed instructions from those who elect them, or representatives, taking into account the views of their electors but also exercising their own judgement. Both are departures from direct democracy where the citizens cast their votes themselves. Despite the coming of the digital economy the need for deliberative institutions which can weigh up evidence and make considered judgements is still a vital component of a healthy democracy. The best way to use the new media is to enable representatives to be more in touch with their electors and more accountable to them. It is impractical for the majority of citizens to acquire the knowledge or spend the time necessary to gain the skills to participate directly in decisionmaking at national, still less at supranational, level. That underlines the point again that democracies only work if voters have trust in the probity and competence of their representatives. Once that is lost much else is lost.

One way of building trust in representatives is to experiment much more with decentralising decisionmaking to local level and encouraging participation of local communities in local decisionmaking. Local government in the UK has been hollowed out over the last 40 years. All parties talk about returning powers to local government but in practice never do, and the finance of local government remains highly centralised in Whitehall. One of the reasons is that central government doubts the competence of local government, and the ability or willingness of local citizens to hold local authorities to account. Many local authorities are closed fiefdoms, in which one party has such a large majority that the city becomes a one-party state. This is a recipe for unaccountable and incompetent government.

Many of the private finance initiative deals that councils have signed are an illustration of this. The Private Finance Initiative (PFI) contract which Sheffield city council signed with Amey corporation to renew the city's roads and pavements was a 25-year contract. It

contained secret clauses only revealed under a freedom of information request, which gave Amey a target of cutting down 17,500
roadside trees, half of the roadside trees in the city, most of which
were healthy and certified as such by an independent tree panel set
up by the council. The council became embroiled in a bitter battle
with residents, protesting at the removal of their trees, and resorted
to strong arm policing, using private security firms and legal injunc-
tions to intimidate protesters. As Nick Clegg said while still an
MP for Sheffield: "The council has lost the plot." If power is to be
decentralised to local councils, citizens need empowering. Directly
elected mayors, proportional representation, forms of deliberative
democracy and a statutory requirement to have proper consultation
with those affected by council policies would all help.

CIVIL SOCIETY

As important as any procedural reforms to how democracy works
are, an Open Left should also be focused on strengthening the ecology of civil society and the quality and extent of the public domain.
A democracy is only as strong as the vitality of the network of voluntary groups and communities which underpins it. David Cameron
for a time promoted the idea of a 'big society' as an alternative to
the state, arguing that there would be no need for state activities if
voluntary groups were invited to fill the gap. The idea fell victim to
austerity. The loading of so many of the spending cuts on to local
government had the unintended consequence that local governments
were forced to cut their grants to voluntary organisations and chari-
ties. The mutual dependence of state and the voluntary sector was
starkly revealed. There are many things the voluntary sector can do
better than the state, but it often needs funding and resources from
the state to be able to do them.

The ecology of civil society also involves ensuring that as wide
a range of companies and other organisations are enabled to exist
as possible. A society is strengthened the greater the variety of

organisations that supply services and provide employment. The way in which the building societies were allowed to shed their mutual status and become banks in the 1990s is a classic example of what to avoid. Many of those new banks collapsed ignominiously in the financial crash in 2008. Local economies need a range of financial institutions and companies, operating at different levels and scales. They need to be protected rather than sacrificed to a uniform model of corporate organisation, which only recognises shareholder value as a legitimate aim. Partnerships such as John Lewis show that it is possible under existing legislation to set up trusts that prevent temporary majorities effecting a change in the nature of the organisation. These legal protections need strengthening and extending, and lessons drawn from other European countries about, for example, small-scale and intermediate-level banking. An Open Left should think hard about how firewalls can be erected around certain types of organisation to preserve vibrant communities and prevent further erosion of their identity. The loss of diversity in the range of shops in many British high streets and shopping malls could be arrested by intelligent regulation.

Attention to the ecology of civil society can play a crucial role in ensuring that communities retain a distinctiveness, sense of pride, local energy and purpose. It heightens a sense of place and belonging, and these are critical elements needed in areas where resentment and a feeling of being left behind is high. External funding is also important, but such areas will not regain their confidence, and will be prone to embrace various forms of populist nationalism, if their civil societies do not revive and start to flourish again. Citizens participate in their democracies in variety of ways; one of the most important is through the many interlinked organisations which make up local communities. It should be a priority of an Open Left to think of practical ways in which assistance and encouragement can be given.

Trade unions are another set of organisations within civil society that need support. Their decline since the 1970s across Europe has weakened progressive movements everywhere because it has removed one of the most powerful demonstrations of the power of collective action and social solidarity. Trade unions cannot be recreated as they were, nor is it desirable that they should be. Many existing unions are highly conservative, hierarchical and male-dominated. Their internal democracies are weak, with very small proportions of their members participating in the governance of their union. Employment patterns have changed radically, but there are many areas, particularly of low-paid and precarious employment, which urgently need the protection and representation that trade unions at their best provide. Forming unions in many parts of the economy is very hard and many obstacles have been erected to make it so. An Open Left should seek to remove those obstacles and create the conditions in which workers who want to join trade unions can do so, and in which new forms of trade unionism can emerge. Strong trade unions were in the past a vital component of a healthy democracy and they can be so again. The pendulum has tilted too far against labour and in favour of capital. Rebuilding democratic and accountable trade unions will help build a more robust wider democracy as well. There need to be many more countervailing powers to the often unchallenged dominance of finance and companies pursuing only shareholder value.

THE PUBLIC DOMAIN

Another concern of an Open Left seeking to strengthen democracy is the public domain, which comprises a range of institutions that define public goods and create the common public spaces and public goods necessary for a thriving democracy. Such institutions include the courts, media, universities, the legislature and the civil service. The public goods most important for democracy are free speech, freedom of association, transparency, accountability, probity and the absence of corruption, and a culture of rational enquiry and policy based on evidence. A strong and secure democracy has many sources of independent criticism and expertise. The Institute for

Fiscal Studies and the Resolution Foundation in London are good examples. If such bodies are respected they can help guide debate. They do not make the choices for politicians or citizens, but explain what different choices entail, and help citizens to make informed judgements. Populist nationalists have no time for such bodies and treat their personnel as part of the global elite who are bent on concealing the truth from the people. They are suspicious of experts and doubt their loyalty. In the populist world you are either one of us or you are an enemy.

The public domain is under pressure from many sources, not just populist nationalists. It always needs defending because corporate interests, for example powerful media groups, often seek to encroach on it and shrink it. One of the most common forms of corruption is the suborning of public institutions by private interests, which can take many forms. Such activities threaten democracy because they lead to politicians and public officials giving higher priority to private interests than to citizens' interests. Preserving a public domain that keeps corruption to the lowest level possible is vital for democracy and to maintain citizens' trust in those who represent and govern them. A country in which even trivial acts of corruption no longer shock or are greeted with a shrug of the shoulders is a country in which democracy is at risk.

The defence of the public domain and its institutions is very important but so too are creative ways of extending and enriching it. An Open Left needs to be concerned with both. We need to be constantly vigilant about the health of our public institutions, their openness, transparency and commitment to the common good. Many of the institutions in the public domain are private institutions, such as newspapers and some TV channels. There are some publicly owned institutions like the BBC and public interest obligations are laid on other news channels. Media organisations have great power and influence, and it is essential that there be sufficient competition between tham so that all views are represented, but also that they operate according to certain standards. We are so fearful of encroaching on freedom of speech that private media are given a wide latitude to operate in whatever way they want. Maintaining a free press is vital, but maintaining the existing ownership rules for the media is not. There should be much more focus on how to create a more diverse and representative media. Concentrations of media ownership should be broken up, and in the wake of the Leveson inquiry tougher rules, particularly on how the press treat ordinary citizens, should be introduced. Like all private companies media companies need to earn their 'license to operate'. There is a public interest in how companies are run and operate, and given the speed with which practices change, it always needs to be kept under review.

There is already considerable regulation of newspapers and broadcasters. Regulation of social media is only just beginning. As with other forms of media the giant companies which have come to dominate social media and the internet have tried to pretend that they only provide a private service for those who sign up to their services, but hardly a week passes without a new revelation of public interest issues arising from how social media is being used. These include terrorism, child sexual abuse, trolling, interference in democratic elections, and the theft and misuse of personal data. If left unchecked the new media will destroy the public domain by undermining its institutions. Regulation of social media in the public interest is urgently needed, so the positive and enriching aspects of it can be preserved. In return for their licence to operate, the companies have to acknowledge their responsibility for the content they host on their platforms and the use that is made of it. The fiction that it is nothing to do with them has to be challenged.

INEQUALITY

There are some established democracies which are already highly inegalitarian and others which are moving in that direction. Should we mind? A formal democracy can coexist with high levels of inequality, but there is a lot of evidence that its citizens will be less happy, trusting and autonomous, all qualities progressives value. Inequality at certain levels breeds resentment and divides societies. Even staff at the IMF now thinks so and advise countries to adopt measures to limit inequality. The more egalitarian a society becomes the easier it is to establish benchmarks of the common good, which provide boundaries within which normal political debate over the best policies can proceed. If societies are very unequal the rich lose contact with the poor and no longer feel any solidarity with them. It is not an accident that the democracies judged most happy are always the Scandinavian countries, which are the least inegalitarian. Rich and poor citizens tend to use the same schools and the same hospitals as everyone else. The quality of public services is very high, as are the levels of tax required to fund them. All the main political parties accept this. One of the consequences is that these societies score highly on trust. Citizens trust one another, and when that is so they are also more likely to trust their political representatives. The Nordic countries have achieved a virtuous circle, although they are far from perfect, and they have their own populist nationalists, such as the True Finns and the Swedish Democrats, who want to bar immigrants and keep the advantages of their welfare states for their own citizens.

An Open Left should not target inequality as a policy goal. It does not need to. We can agree with the defenders of inequality that the rise of inequality in recent decades has been a byproduct of policies, such as deregulation, privatisation, lower taxes and open markets, rather than aimed at directly. The great reduction in inequality which took place in the postwar years was also a byproduct of the pursuit of other policies, the policies which extended the welfare state and the regulation of capitalism. If inequality is to be reduced again in the decades to come it will be as a result of renewed commitment to the principles of a universal welfare state and an inclusive economy, as the Nordic countries demonstrate so clearly.

Other kinds of inequality are different. One of the most important and long-standing progressive causes has been ending discrimination and building a society in which everyone's rights are respected and all citizens are treated equally. Extending civil, political and social rights to all citizens has always been one of the great engines of progressive politics. Despite the significant achievements of the past, such as the abolition of slavery and votes for women, there is still so much more to do. It is 100 years since the first bill giving votes to women was passed, but it is only now that there are beginning to be sizeable numbers of women in parliament and the cabinet, and even then still well below half. The Equal Pay Act was passed almost 50 years ago, yet progress towards achieving equal pay has been glacial. The exposure of institutional biases on gender and race in so many public institutions has revealed how widespread and deeply ingrained discriminatory practices remain. They have often been protected by a lack of transparency. Once the facts are disclosed the case for change is compelling for most people. It is a reminder of one of the key pillars of an effective public domain: where rights of citizens are concerned everything should be out in the open, so that there is nowhere to hide, and the secrecy which protects privilege can be broken. But no one should underestimate what a struggle it has been to get this far, and how much further there is to go.

THE WAY AHEAD

After the battering that progressive ideals and progressive causes have had in the years since the financial crash can we sense a new beginning? We need a vision and a new strategy for the 2020s and beyond. New opportunities are opening. After a decade of austerity and slow recovery, 10 years of defeats and reverses, and the growth of populist nationalisms as well as authoritarian nationalisms around the world, can we start hoping for better times?

There are many reasons why we should be cautious. Pessimism of the intellect, optimism of the will was Gramsci's advice. He did not counsel optimism of the intellect. We need the most sober realistic assessment of our predicament and our prospects that we can get. Otherwise we risk exaggerating what is possible and enter a world of illusion. We need to be clear-eyed about the continuing risks we face. Another major crash in the international economy is possible. There are still a savings glut, huge imbalances, very high levels of unsecured debt, and a great deal of reckless behaviour in the financial markets. The possibility exists that we will have to endure another meltdown, another recession, renewed austerity before the conditions for a new boom are created. It is not certain, but many analysts of the markets think it likely. There are still too many things that could go wrong and have not been fixed from last time. On top of this there are serious risks to international cooperation. The world has been moving in a markedly protectionist direction since 2008, and with Trump and his economic nationalist doctrines becoming increasingly ascendant in Washington, this looks set to continue. An all-out trade war between the US on one side and China and the EU on the other is still avoidable, but it is coming perilously closer. Countries outside the big blocs have reason to be fearful.

If there is another cataclysm the western international order may not survive it. Globalisation could then really go into reverse and a world of regional trade blocs will loom. The potential dislocation to world trade is immense if the US is serious about starting a trade war with China. A large part of the US trade deficit with China comes from US corporations like Apple operating in China and selling back into the US. The intricate production chains which have sprung up in the last 30 years would be disrupted. China might retaliate by refusing to fund any longer the US trillion dollar debt, which could lead to a collapse of the dollar. The shockwaves this would send through the international economy would be immense. The former US treasury secretary and economist Larry Summers warned before Trump was elected that if he tried to follow through on his protectionist instincts the result would be a world depression. The chance of that has risen considerably in 2018.

There are wider dangers to the international order arising from the intensification of great power rivalries, particularly between the US, China, India and Russia. The EU's civilian power model of multilateral engagement will struggle in such a world (the UK's Global Britain model will struggle even to breathe). It will force the EU to become more like a great power itself if it is to survive. The alternative is a steady balkanisation of the EU, which has already begun with the UK's decision to leave. This is a world very much desired by Russia, which wants to destroy the rules-based international system and in its place put bilateral bargaining between strong regional powers, with control over their immediate regions as their main spheres of interest, while supporting client states and engaging in proxy wars elsewhere.

If this was not enough there are the grave perils of climate change and nuclear proliferation. Multilateral negotiations were making some headway on both, but their future has been thrown into doubt by Trump's espousal of unilateralism, and his repudiation of deals signed by his predecessors. If the US withdraws from the rules-based system it will be greatly weakened, and any progress on the big global challenges facing the world will have to proceed on bilateral lines or within nation states and regional blocs themselves. One of the big uncertainties raised by Trump's chaotic tenure of the White House is whether this is an aberration in US policy, or whether it signals a long-term shift in the orientation of the US to the rest of the world.

It is easy to be depressed by the recent turn of events. But we must remember the other side. The world economy has been transformed in the last 30 years and that is not going to be reversed. The rising powers are better placed than western economies to survive a new recession and will emerge still stronger. Not many of these countries are democracies, but from a progressive perspective it is an important advance to see so many people lifted out of poverty, and the possibility that in the next stage many African countries will become involved as well. The potential of the digital economy is immense. We have already been amazed by some of the changes it has made and there are likely to be many more of those in the next 20 years. Possible developments in green energy, medicine and robotics offer the possibility of a more secure future for all the peoples of the planet. The scope and the need for multilateral cooperation has never been greater. There is a prize here which all progressives can recognise.

Progress has never been linear. It has always been a deeply contradictory process, profoundly disillusioning for many people who believe so passionately in trying to make the world a better place. It has always been like this. Those sceptical about progress, like the philosopher John Gray, think that our mistake is to believe in the possibility of progress at all. He believes the world never gets better, or if it does, it soon relapses. Human life goes in cycles not straight lines. Almost everyone before modernity used to think like this. Gray debunks the great modern illusion that we can take control of our fate. On the other side, the psychologist Steven Pinker insists that the institutions of modernity have enabled human societies to engineer measurable and significant improvements to the conditions under which the majority live their lives. These are two very different accounts of our world. Progressives are naturally drawn to Pinker's optimism, but they also need a regular dose of Gray's scepticism and realism to keep their feet on the ground.

An Open Left needs to draw on both perspectives on modernity in fashioning its project for the 2020s. It should be committed to openness, rationality, inclusiveness and pluralism. It seeks to construct a progressive order, which can give protection to citizens and also provide opportunity. The problems and the obstacles are glaring and obvious. The orders we rely on – whether international governance, capitalist market economies, universal welfare states or representative democracy – are deeply flawed. When you add in the looming environmental crisis the human species appears to be in a race against itself to avert catastrophe. HG Wells thought at the beginning of the 20th century that only education would stop human beings destroying themselves. We still need education, but we need other things too – a more inclusive and greener economy, a turn back to multilateral rule-based international governance, a renewed commitment to universal welfare states, and a democratic culture which generates trust. Will we get all this? Of course not, but we can set a direction.

PROGRESSIVE NARRATIVES

In developing an Open Left for Britain we can draw on the rich vein of progressive traditions in Britain stretching back over more than 200 years, and also on the experience of other parts of Europe and across the world. An Open Left must be prepared to learn lessons and reflect critically about what worked and what did not work, or may no longer work, in progressive experiments and projects in the past. One of the problems which has always beset progressive politics is that progressives too easily dissolve into tribes fighting one another instead of seeking what they have in common, building alliances and cooperating. In the UK the progressive tradition has been dominated in the 20th century by Labour and the Labour tradition. This has been a very rich experience, but also a restrictive one: Labour has only succeeded on three occasions in its history in assembling a broad progressive coalition capable of winning a parliamentary majority and implementing a progressive programme. The Labour movement has at times absorbed many progressives from other parties and movements, particularly the Liberals, but it has shed many too. There has often been an exclusiveness about Labour which has limited its appeal. Labour also embraced a notion of progress, the forward march of Labour, which treated Labour's advance and ultimate victory as inevitable. As the great majority of citizens were working class it was only a matter of time before the weight of numbers delivered governments that would implement socialism. The early disappointments and setbacks which Labour experienced were made easier to accept by the comforting belief that it would all work out to Labour's advantage in the end. A prudent, step-by-step approach was the right way forward.

The problem with Labour's approach, as the historian Eric Hobsbawm pointed out in the 1980s, was that it was fatalistic. It assumed the future was guaranteed, but this assumption rested on a conception of the world which was rapidly being undermined. Organised labour movements, although a very powerful force across Europe, were never strong enough on their own to become the majority. They always needed allies even at the height of their strength, and when that strength began to decline, as industrial employment fell and trade unions were weakened, so the need to reach beyond their base became essential if the principles for which they stood were to be realised.

Hobsbawm's point was that a narrow class politics in an increasingly complex modern democracy misread the nature of the society and kind of coalition that would be necessary to achieve a government committed to a broad progressive programme. This is a general lesson progressives have often had to relearn. No group can claim an exclusive right over how to define what is to count as progress. It has to be determined in every generation afresh. Ramsay MacDonald, Labour's first prime minister, understood the strengths but also the weaknesses of a Labour movement that was rooted in class politics and class identity, contending for power in a democracy in which that kind of class politics and class identity was not sufficient to win a majority. MacDonald endeavoured to persuade his party to see itself as a 'Great Labour party', the successor to the 'Great Liberal party' of the 19th century, which had been the party of progress, able to appeal to all parts of the progressive coalition. The Labour movement was for a time enrolled within it. The counter tradition in the party argued that Labour should be a class party, because the working class was the majority, and the task was to persuade all working-class people to identify with their class party.

MacDonald did not have much success persuading his party. He never won a parliamentary majority, formed two short-lived minority governments and then abandoned the progressive cause and his party in the cataclysm of 1931. But although he became a non-person in the party his project lived on. In 1945 and 1966 Labour won power as a national rather than a class party, constructing a coalition which had the Labour movement at its heart but went beyond it, setting out a national vision for economic and social renewal, which attracted voters with progressive principles from all parties. Both governments implemented a progressive programme, but only lasted in office six years. They were overwhelmed partly by events and partly by internal divisions and poor strategic choices. They failed to consolidate and build on the foundations they had laid and establish a lasting progressive hegemony. The Attlee government is much more celebrated today than the Wilson government, but at the time both were heavily criticised from the left, reflecting deep schisms in the party about policy and electoral strategy, and led to prolonged civil wars, which played their part in keeping Labour out of government. It is important to study the Attlee and Wilson governments to understand their progressive achievements and also why they were not able to achieve more, and why their electoral success was limited.

The third majority government that Labour has so far produced, the New Labour administration formed by Tony Blair and Gordon Brown in 1997, was the most successful government in electoral terms in Labour's history. It was re-elected three times, the first two by landslides, and served three full terms. Yet today this is the most reviled government and Blair the most reviled former Labour leader, apart from MacDonald. In time this will change, because New Labour achieved far more than some of its critics allow, and its successes and failures need to be taken into account too, alongside the successes and failures of Labourism, Croslandite revisionism, and state socialism for the project of an Open Left.

In this book I have identified that project as having four main priorities. The first priority is an open multilateral international order, which is built on defending and developing the multilateral institutions we already have both at the global level, including the UN, the IMF and the World Bank, and at the regional level, including the EU, Mercosur and Asean. At the same time, we must recognise the need to go beyond the western-centric order of the past and fully involve the rising powers in Asia, Africa and South America in determining the rules that should govern this order. Enhancing the role of the G20 is one way to start doing this. Failure to maintain multilateral institutions will endanger the security of the whole world by risking a return to economic nationalism and military adventurism.

The second priority is an inclusive and sustainable economy, based on reorienting our economic thinking away from the pursuit of economic growth at any cost and the maximisation of shareholder value to what is required to safeguard the biosphere and maximise value for all stakeholders, particularly domestic households and local economies. There is a wealth of new economic thinking on the progressive left, and running through it is an appreciation that the next economic model – in seeking to rebalance the economy, and tackle the problems of climate change and of places left behind by globalisation – will need to strengthen and extend state capacities to make possible a more decentralised, egalitarian and sharing economy and to encourage the emergence of new forms of enterprise. Local economies need more insulation from the globalised sectors of the economy, and economic activities should be judged as to how they maximise stakeholder value rather than shareholder value.

The third priority is a remodeled welfare state, based on a new commitment to universal basic services to provide households with security, through income support, and opportunity, through investment in education, health and care, ensuring that no one is left behind. Citizens have to be persuaded to pay more for the many benefits they receive from public services that make up modern welfare states, and providers need to experiment with delivering their services in more local and decentralised ways. Hypothecated taxes, living wages, equal investment in all 16–20-year-olds, and capital grants are all ideas that should be explored further.

The fourth priority is a renewed democracy, based on defending the basic institutions that have come to define democracy, including the rule of law, equal rights for all citizens, media plurality, freedom of association and freedom of speech. This should be complemented by tackling the many new threats, including the erosion of trust in representatives and experts, the eruption of social media, and the weakening of communities. A fair and proportional voting system is overdue. So too is decentralisation of power to ensure real local accountability and more local participation in decisionmaking about local economies, the needs of households and the protection of the biosphere. The quest for equal citizenship, targeting the many forms of discrimination, disadvantage and abuse which still damage so many lives, remains central to the progressive project.

There is no single progressive party, no single will of the people or of the class that progressives can lean on in developing projects for change. We live in complex post-industrial economies and multicultural societies. Opinions, interests and knowledge are all divided, and the old certainties and landmarks have disappeared.

An Open Left has to acknowledge that there are many values and perspectives, and no single right way. That is the first step necessary to forming a new progressive coalition. There needs to be as well a realism about the problems and challenges ahead, as well as realism about voters, and how best to construct a coalition that can form a government. Progressive parties have always pitched their appeal disproportionately to the young and there are good reasons for that. The older generations tend to be more conservative because the material interests they have acquired make them risk-averse when it comes to politics. But although the current youth generation, particularly students, is more than ever moving left and championing progressive causes, as the 2017 election in the UK showed, a winning coalition cannot be built on the votes of the young alone, particularly since they remain much less likely to vote than the old. A progressive party, as in 1945, 1966 and 1997, has to make an appeal that crosses the generations as it crosses the classes. The task is to present a new and convincing national vision of what is wrong with the country and what has to be done to put it right, and to convince voters that the party of progress has a leadership that can be trusted to be competent and honest. There is a very substantial party of progress in Britain as there is throughout Europe. The challenge is to forge the alliances to unite it under one banner. Constructing an Open Left is a first step.

GUIDE TO FURTHER READING

There is a wealth of writing about the issues and themes raised in this book. What follows is not a comprehensive guide to the literature, which would be another book in itself, but a listing of some of the books and sources I have found most useful in writing this book, and which I hope may be useful to others.

For a restatement of the idea of progress it is hard to beat Steven Pinker's *Enlightenment Now: The Case for Reason, Science, Humanism and Progress* (London: Penguin 2017). For the sceptical case see John Gray's *Gray's Anatomy: Selected Writings* (London: Penguin 2013). Furio Cerutti dissects the double-edged nature of progress in *Global Challenges for Leviathan: A Political Philosophy of Nuclear Weapons and Global Warming* (Lanham, MD: Lexington Books 2007). For an antidote to pessimism see Rutger Bregman's *Utopia for Realists: And How We Can Get There* (London: Bloomsbury 2017). I discussed the nature of politics and the idea of progress in *Politics and Fate* (Cambridge: Polity 2000).

One of the best recent books on the future of the left is Andrew Hindmoor's *What's Left Now? The History and Future of Social Democracy* (Oxford: Oxford University Press 2018). Eric Hobsbawm's seminal essay *The Forward March of Labour Halted?* (London: NLB 1981) is still worth consulting. For earlier phases of the debates around the strategy of the British Labour party see David Marquand's *Ramsay MacDonald* (London: Richard Cohen Books 1997), Ralph Miliband's *Parliamentary Socialism* (London: Merlin 1964) and Patrick Diamond's *The Crosland Legacy: The Future of British Social Democracy* (Bristol: Policy Press 2016), and for later phases see Tony Giddens' *The Third Way* (Cambridge: Polity 1998) and *Third Way and Its Critics* (Cambridge: Polity 2000). The electoral position of the British Labour party has been analysed by Patrick Diamond and Charlie Cadywould in *Don't Forget the Middle: How Labour Can Build a New Centre-left Majority* (London: Policy Network 2017).

An essential starting point for thinking about globalisation is Immanuel Wallerstein's *The Modern World System* (London: Academic Press 1976). Contemporary globalisation was analysed by David Held, Anthony McGrew, David Goldblatt and Jonathan Perraton in *Global Transformations* (Cambridge: Polity 1999). The continuing importance of nation states was argued by Paul Hirst and Grahame Thompson in *Globalisation in Question* (Cambridge: Polity 1996). A key text on the current problems of globalisation and the backlash against it is Dani Rodrik's *The Globalisation Paradox* (Oxford: OUP 2011).

The new populism, or populist nationalism as I prefer to characterise it, already has a large literature. Especially useful are Jan-Werner Muller's *What Is Populism?* (Philadelphia: University of Pennsylvania Press 2016), Cas Mudde and Cristóbal Kaltwasser's *Populism: A Very Short Introduction* (New York: OUP 2017), and Jan Zielonka's *Counter Revolution: Liberal Europe in Retreat* (Oxford: OUP 2018). An insight into the economic nationalism of Donald Trump is provided by Charlie Laderman and Brendan Simms in *Donald Trump: The Making of a World View* (London: Endeavour Press 2017).

The growth of global governance networks reflecting the extent of interdependence which has developed in the globalisation era is analysed by Anne-Marie Slaughter in *A New World Order* (Princeton: Princeton University Press 2009). An overview of the reforms to global governance which are now needed is provided by Colin Hay and Tony Payne in *Civic Capitalism* (Cambridge: Polity 2015). On the EU as a regional order see Mario Telò, *Europe A Civilian Power? EU, Global Governance and World Order* (London: Palgrave-Macmillan 2005) and *Regionalism in Hard Times Competitive and Post-liberal Trends in Europe, Asia, Africa and the Americas* (London: Routledge 2016). For a pessimistic view of the problems of the eurozone see David Marsh's *Europe's Deadlock: How It Could Be Solved and Why It Won't Happen* (London: Yale University Press 2013). On security and defence see Douglas Alexander and Ian Kearns (eds), *Influencing Tomorrow: Future Challenges for British Foreign Policy* (London: Guardian Books 2013). The transcript of Robin Cook's resignation speech in the House of Commons in 2003 is available at https://publications.parliament.uk/pa/cm200203/cmhansrd/vo030317/debt-ext/30317-33.htm and the video can be found at https://www.c-span.org/video/?175547-4/cook-resignation-speech.

There are many important contributions to the debate on what a new economic model for the UK should be. Two of the most valuable are Colin Hay and Tony Payne (eds), *Civic Capitalism* (Cambridge: Polity 2015) and Michael Jacobs and Mariana Mazzucato (eds), *Rethinking Capitalism: Economics and Policy for Sustainable and Inclusive Growth* (London: John Wiley 2016). Colin Crouch has also written several important recent books, including *Making Capitalism Fit for Society* (Cambridge: Polity 2013). The Centre for Research on Socio-Cultural Change (CRESC) at the University of Manchester has spearheaded the analysis of the 'foundational economy'. Rachel Reeves' pamphlet on the 'everyday economy' can be found at https://www.scribd.com/document/374425087/Rachel-Reeves-The-Everyday-Economy. For Ruth Pearson's analysis of the reproductive economy see 'Plan F: A Feminist Economics Strategy for Post-crisis Britain' in Johnna Montgomerie (ed), *Forging Economic Discovery in 21st Century Britain* (London: PERC, Goldsmiths, University of London 2015). The same collection has an article by Michael Moran summarising the CRESC conception of the foundational economy. The idea of moral economy in progressive thought has recently been explored by Tim Rogan in *The Moral Economists* (Princeton: Princeton University Press 2017).

Ian Gough has written an indispensable guide to climate change and environmental risks in *Heat, Greed and Human Need: Climate Change, Capitalism and Sustainable Well-being* (Cheltenham: Edward Elgar 2017). For a progressive green economic strategy see the analysis in *Rethinking Capitalism* by Michael Jacobs and also Tony Giddens' *The Politics of Climate Change* (Cambridge: Polity 2011).

The financial crash and its aftermath is analysed by Wolfgang Streeck in *How Will Capitalism End?* (London: Verso 2016). For austerity see Mark Blyth, *Austerity: The History of a Dangerous Idea* (Oxford: Oxford University Press 2016) and Yanis Varoufakis *And the Weak Suffer What They Must? Europe, Austerity and the Threat to Global Stability* (London: Bodley Head 2016). The impact on living standards in the UK has been documented in pioneering work by the Resolution Foundation in a series of reports, while the most authoritative source for fiscal impacts is the Institute for Fiscal Studies. A valuable analysis of the recession is Tom Clark's *Hard Times: Inequality, Recession, Aftermath* (London: Yale University Press 2014). See also the study by Guy Standing, *The Precariat: The New Dangerous Class* (London: Bloomsbury 2014).

The thesis of secular stagnation owes much to the work of Robert Gordon in *Is US Economic Growth Over? Faltering Innovation Confronts the Six Headwinds* (nber.org 2012). See also Tyler Cowen, *The Great Stagnation* (New York: Dutton 2011). Anatole Kaletsky is much more optimistic in *Capitalism 4.0: The Birth of a New Economy* (London: Bloomsbury 2010). The potential of the new economy is explored and its capacity to transform society and politics in Nick Srnicek, *Inventing the Future: Postcapitalism and a World Without Work* (London: Verso 2016), Eric Brynjolfsson and Andrew McAfee, *The Second Machine Age: Work, Progress and Prosperity in a Time of Brilliant Technologies* (New York: Norton 2016) and Paul Mason, *Post-capitalism: A Guide to Our Future* (London:

Penguin 2016). There is also a wealth of information and analysis on the future of work and the implications of the new digital economy on the web pages of the RSA. See particularly some of the blogs by Matthew Taylor, especially https://www.thersa.org/discover/ publications-and-articles/matthew-taylor-blog/2015/09/grasping-the-future--why-progressives-must-champion-the-human-potential-of-the-digital-economy/. For Charlie Leadbeater's ideas of how the sharing economy could transform all our lives see http://www.the-guardian.com/politics/2015/jul/12/14-ideas-that-could-save-labour/.

Corporate governance is a neglected field on the progressive left. The place to start is John Parkinson's magisterial book *Corporate Power and Responsibility: Issues in the Theory of Company Law* (Oxford: Oxford University Press 1994). See also John Parkinson, Gavin Kelly and Andrew Gamble (eds), *The Political Economy of the Company* (London: Bloomsbury 2001). Will Hutton has highlighted the shortcomings of UK corporate governance in a number of major works on political economy, which deal with many of the themes of this book, starting with *The State We're In* (London: Cape 1994) and most recently *How Good We Can Be: Ending the Mercenary Society and Building a Great Country* (London: Little, Brown 2015).

The current dilemmas and prospects of the welfare state are explored by Anton Hemerijck in *Changing Welfare States* (Oxford: Oxford University Press 2013), Peter Taylor-Gooby in *The Double Crisis of the Welfare State and What We Can Do About It* (London: Palgrave-Macmillan 2013), John Hills in *Good Times, Bad Times: The Welfare Myth of Them and Us* (Bristol: Policy Press 2015), and Colin Hay and Daniel Wincott in *The Political Economy of European Welfare Capitalisms* (London: Palgrave-Macmillan 2012). Paul Pierson's earlier gloomy prognostications can be found in *The New Politics of the Welfare State* (Oxford: Oxford University Press 2001). Among the many journalists commenting on the welfare state, Polly Toynbee's columns for *The Guardian* stand out.

The work of the Social Mobility Commission has been important in collating up-to-date evidence on what is happening to social mobility, particularly since the crash and the recession. Their reports can be accessed on their website. Inequality has been explored by Thomas Piketty in *Capital in the Twenty-first Century* (Cambridge, MA: Harvard University Press 2014) and by Tony Atkinson in *Inequality* (Cambridge, MA: Harvard University Press 2015). Branko Milanovi has written a major study of globalisation and inequality – *Global Inequality: A New Approach for the Age of Globalisation* (Cambridge, MA: Harvard University Press 2016). For generational inequality see David Willetts' *The Pinch: How the Babyboomers Took Their Children's Future and Why They Should Give It Back* (London: Atlantic Books 2011).

Universal basic income is explored by Louise Haagh in *The Case for Basic Income* (Cambridge: Polity 2018) and by Anthony Painter at http://basicincome.org/news/2017/02/anthony-painter-universal-basic-income-answer-poverty-insecurity-health-inequality/. For the alternative idea of universal basic services see the report by Henrietta Moore and Jonathan Portes: https://www.ucl.ac.uk/bartlett/igp/news/2017/oct/igps-social-prosperity-network-publishes-uks-first-report-universal-basic-services. Capital grants as a way of countering wealth inequality and improving social mobility and personal autonomy have been explored by Bruce Ackerman and Anne Alstott in *The Stakeholder Society* (New Haven, CT: Yale University Press 2008) and Rajiv Rajiv Prabhakar ub *The Assets Agenda: Principles and Policy* (London: Palgrave-Macmillan 2008). A new Institute for Public Policy Research (IPPR) report on capital grants available at https://www.ippr.org/research/publications/our-common-wealth continues the earlier pioneering work at IPPR by Gavin Kelly and Will Paxton.

David Runciman points out the shortcomings but also the resilience of representative democracy in *The Confidence Trap: A History of Democracy in Crisis from World War 1 to the Present* (Princeton: Princeton University Press 2013) and *How Democracy Ends* (London: Profile Books 2018). Stein Ringen suggests ways in which we can compare democracies in *What Democracy Is For: On Freedom and Moral Government* (Princeton: Princeton University Press 2009). Albert Weale criticises attacks on representative democracy and the shallowness of populism in *The Will of the People: A Modern Myth* (Cambridge: Polity 2018). Simon Tormey puts the case for moving beyond representative democracy in *The End of Representative Politics* (Cambridge: Polity 2015).

The shortcomings of representative democracy and political parties in promoting full equality of citizens' rights are exposed by Joni Lovenduski in 'Feminist reflections on representative democracy' in Andrew Gamble and Tony Wright (eds) *Rethinking Democracy* (Oxford: Wiley-Blackwell 2018) and by Owen Jones, arguing passionately that progressives must not tolerate any form of discrimination against minorities at https://www.facebook.com/owenjones84/videos/1663640047062834/.

There has been for some time a lively debate about the causes of citizens' disengagement from politics. Some of the key texts are Gerry Stoker, *Why Politics Matters: Making Democracy Work* (London: Palgrave-Macmillan 2006); Matthew Flinders, *Defending Politics: Why Democracy Matters in the 21st Century* (Oxford: Oxford University Press 2013); and Colin Hay, *Why We Hate Politics* (Cambridge: Polity 2007). Two authoritative recent works on the British constitution from different standpoints are Vernon Bogdanor's *The New British Constitution* (London: Hart 2009) and Anthony King's *The British Constitution* (Oxford: Oxford University Press 2010). The issues around the media in modern democracy are explored by Thomas Meyer in *Media Democracy: How the Media Colonise Politics* (Cambridge: Polity 2002) and by Martin Moore in *Democracy Hacked: Political Turmoil and Information Warfare in the Digital Age* (London: OneWorld Publications 2018).

Immigration is examined by Andrew Geddes and Peter Scholten in *The Politics of Migration and Immigration in Europe* (London: Sage 2016). Two different standpoints in the debate are demonstrated in David Goodhart's *The British Dream: Successes and Failures of Post-war Immigration* (London: Atlantic Books 2013) and Harvey Redgrave's report for the Institute for Global Change, *Balanced Migration: A Progressive Approach*, https://institute.global/insight/renewing-centre/balanced-migration-progressive-approach.

John Harris explores what might be needed to reinvigorate and rebuild trade unionism in the UK in a Guardian article at https://www.theguardian.com/commentisfree/2018/mar/19/new-breed-trade-union-rmt-unite-unison.

Overcentralisation in the British system of government and the need for a radical decentralisation to counter disengagement and alienation from politics has long been a theme of Gerry Stoker's work. He summarises his argument in 'Relating and responding to the politics of resentment' in Andrew Gamble and Tony Wright (eds), *Rethinking Democracy* (Oxford: Wiley-Blackwell 2018). For the Preston model see Aditya Chakrabortty, https://www.theguardian.com/commentisfree/2018/jan/31/preston-hit-rock-bottom-took-back-control.

Details of the campaign to save the trees in Sheffield can be found at https://savesheffieldtrees.org.uk/. There is a link to a BBC video here and also the text of a statement issued by Sheffield TUC: https://www.facebook.com/BBCPolitics/videos/2179193938764119/?hc_ref=ARQdesn9k6jPhrRtRFwvXwKXVAz58oa2eG9jT233DDBJ83KH_1y97SFknzK6QEI9VtA&pnref=story.

The following amended motion was agreed at Sheffield TUC Delegate Meeting on Tuesday night 27 March 2018 after a good debate. The original motion was submitted by UNITE NE 403/5 N4P Branch:

Sheffield TUC opposes the consequences of the PFI deal for street improvements in Sheffield which has led to both widespread removal of the trees and the failure to meet the timescales for road improvements. If this work had been delivered in-house by a council service, the trees management programme could have been managed with a discussion with local residents and tree campaigners.

As it is, the actions of Amy plc have both failed the council's road improvement ambitions and undermined the reputation of Sheffield's environmental credentials.

We welcome the recent decision to pause the tree felling which is causing unacceptable levels of disputation.

We call on the Sheffield Labour Group to support the immediate, mediated settlement to the felling of Sheffield's street trees and a reappraisal of the Amey contract with a view to bringing it back in house as a municipally owned direct works operation as soon as possible.

We support the GMB members at Amey PLC in their current dispute with their employers regarding their pay and conditions and health and safety concerns.

We also call for an immediate cessation of the use of private security guards and police, particularly their use of heavy handed tactics against protestors which has shocked not only Sheffield citizens, but has caused appalling negative publicity nationally for the city.

(Martin Mayer, Secretary, Sheffield TUC)